UBUNTU
CRADLES OF PEACE AND DEVELOPMENT

(Ed) Alewyn P Burger

KAGISO
PUBLISHERS

UBUNTU Cradles of peace and development

Copyright © Kagiso Publishers 1996
Masada Building, cor. Proes & Paul Kruger Streets, Pretoria 0002
PO Box 629, Pretoria 0001

Bloemfontein • Cape Town • Durban • King William's Town • Mmabatho •
Nelspruit • Pietersburg • Port Elizabeth • Pretoria • Umtata

First edition, first impression 1996/03

Typeset by Cuneiform Graphics
Printed and bound by ABC Press (Pty) Ltd, 21 Kinghall Avenue,
Epping II, Cape Town 7460

ISBN 0-7986-4264-5

Contents

Declaration
  • The message of this Declaration
  1. Preamble
  2. Background
  3. The aim: peace and development
  4. The cradles of peace and development: where attitudes are shaped
  5. Postscript

Author index

PREFACE

The great gift God has given South Africa is her people. Their love of life, their penchant for all the good things that God created us to enjoy – laughter, love, singing and dancing. All activities that are shared in community. Although the majority of our people may amount to very little materially, they are rich beyond bounds in their deep-rooted togetherness. A sharing and caring for each other in adversity – as well as in the good times. In Xhosa the word is *Ubuntu* – difficult to translate, but essentially meaning that a person only becomes a person through other people.

It is this recognition of a need for each other that gives hope to our country. It is an emphasis on the positive in seemingly hopeless situations. This collection of essays expands on this theme. Development can only come about through a recognition of our interdependence. We need each other and it is through working together that we are going to achieve a peaceful and prosperous new South Africa.

God bless you

Desmond M. Tutu
Archbishop of South Africa

Organisers' preface

Violence and the threat of its escalation surrounded the approach to the democratic general election of 1994 - yet, miraculously, it went well. These circumstances emphasised the importance of the pursuit of peace and development.

South Africa's diversity can either be wonderfully enriching, or racial, ethnic and other tensions can be a curse that aggravates all other problems and destroys the fabric of society.

Against this background, the need was felt for a conference to focus attention on the fostering of attitudes that will bring peace and development. Attitudes are formed from childhood in the basic institutions of society, such as the family, the church and the school. The purpose was thus to work towards a 'blueprint' for enlisting the contributions of these and other institutions towards ensuring peace and development.

The conference took place from 2 to 5 November 1994 at the University of Pretoria's Conference Centre. A distinguished panel of local and foreign speakers addressed about a hundred committed and active delegates, hailing from eight of the nine provinces, and from two neighbouring and three overseas countries.

The initiative came from the Institute of World Concerns (IWC), a non-profit organisation, founded in the UK in 1990 to stimulate interdisciplinary exchange on issues that threaten humanity, and to promote genuine moral convictions. The two co-patrons were the National Peace Committee, which contributed significantly towards creating a peaceful climate during the negotiation process and the April 1994 elections, and the University of South Africa, the largest university in southern Africa, traditionally serving all population groups.

The conference was aimed at an interdisciplinary exchange for a wide audience, with the emphasis on moral values. It also became a major contribution to South Africa's participation in the International Year of the Family. The approach was similar to that of the previous IWC conference in South Africa, in November 1992, entitled *AIDS and Your Response*, which followed in the wake of the National AIDS Convention of South Africa (NACOSA).

The topics dealt with in the papers and working group discusions range from local experience to lessons to be learnt from other countries; from consideration of evil and morality to practical situations; from reconciliation in general to the role of specific groups such as the youth. Concentrated coverage was given to five areas, namely, the twofold ultimate aims of obtaining peace and development, and domains viewed as 'cradles' of peace and development, notably the three domains of the family, the church and the school. Hence the conference title, *The Cradles of Peace and Development*.

The speakers were people from all population groups and both genders, of a variety of expertise, representing different philosophical, political and religious views, and including two Africans from neighbouring countries and three African-Americans.

This volume contains the papers presented. While the patrons do not necessarily agree with the contents of all papers and comments, the diversity gives expression to the IWC's approach of stimulating cross-pollination intended to lead to innovative and effective action and changes.

The papers are given here in the order of presentation in the programme. This order was dictated by the need to have material in all five of the areas mentioned, for discussion in the working groups on the second and again on the third day.

The first night centred round an opening address by Mr John Hall, the chairperson of the National Peace Committee, and the keynote address by Mr Bryn Jones, founding Director of the IWC. It also afforded a suitable opportunity for a statement by Mr Alan Scotland, chairman of IWC, and for thanking and receiving messages from the co-patrons and the Department of Welfare, a major sponsor.

Then followed two days of the delivery of authoritative papers by experts from varying backgrounds, with time for questions and comments after each session. Each day ended with speakers and delegates participating in the working groups of their choice, covering the five broad areas of the conference theme.

The world première of a TV documentary entitled *The miracle of South Africa*, depicting the way in which the threat of uncontrollable violence in the approach to the general election was averted, took place on the last morning. This gripping programme, directed by the Belgian TV producer Juul Claes, was offered by Alabanza Media and introduced by Ms Dini Esterhuizen.

Also on the last morning, the facilitators of the working groups reported back on their deliberations and recommendations. These reports, together with the papers delivered, served as a basis for the closing synthesis by Dr Keri Jones, and also for drawing up the Declaration.

After the conference, the initial draft Declaration was submitted to all the speakers and the Organising Committee for their comments. Over several months, through many comments and various input to ensure that the ethos of the conference was properly reflected, the final form emerged. The title chosen is *Ubuntu! Love your neighbour in diversity,* which tries to express the heart of its message. We hope that it will help transform people's thinking towards respect for human dignity and moral values, and lead to decisive actions that will put communities in motion.

The Declaration appears at the end of this volume, and is also being distributed widely as a separate document, soliciting input from the public on the issues dealt with. Such input will be essential to arrive at well-defined actions and targets, and to identify key functionaries who will act to achieve the stated objectives.

On the last day, delegates were invited to submit their candid written comments on the conference. Prominently displayed in these was personal commitment to the conference's message. One delegate said: "I think we got more than a 'Declaration' - we got individual and collective commitment to do what we could to strengthen the cradles of peace and development." A moving aspect was that five delegates described their experience of the conference in superlative terms: "the highlight of my life", "the best thing that has ever happened to me", "the most illuminating I have ever attended", "the best conference I have ever attended", "the most meaningful one of the many conferences which I have attended and participated in during my lifetime".

What remains, is the implementation of what has emerged from this conference. That is what the Declaration is intended to facilitate, and we hope that to many it will become a reference manual and a household word. Its message is one of moral values and respect for human dignity, of justice and righteousness in all spheres of life. Our community is challenged in respect of all facets of the conference theme:
- Peace demands a strong commitment from all, in the light of demonstrated inherent evil
- Development has to be rooted in a sound community of properly functioning sub-communities
- The family epitomises the value of caring relationships
- The church must show itself to be the strongest moral force in the community, by accepting its reconciliation task
- The school must equip people with both character and life skills.

In actions of implementation this proceedings volume can serve as a reference, as can the audio and video recordings of the proceedings. Copies can be ordered from the Institute of World Concerns in South Africa, the United Kingdom or the United States of America at the addresses given below.

Thanks are due to everyone who contributed to the success of the first part of this venture: Bryn and Keri Jones and Alan Scotland for their moral support and substantial contribution to the planning and execution; the three co-patron bodies who lent identity to the effort; Cilla Taylor, Ammie Wissing and Alyson Lea-Cox of Conference Planners in Irene who did most of the hard work; the members of the Organising Committee for constructive thinking and active assistance; the sponsors, listed in the Declaration, for showing concern in a vitally important area; the speakers, chairmen and facilitators for the most valuable content of the papers, discussions and reports; Dini Esterhuizen for the production and showing of *The Miracle of South Africa;* the venue operators and caterers for good facilities and service; the media and audio and video operators for their valuable service; the delegates for their constructive involvement; and many others who served selflessly at various stages of the preparation, publicity and execution.

Regarding the follow-up phase - which is still continuing - there is a growing list of people to whom thanks are due. Eddie Harvey and his staff at the Department of Welfare extended their sponsorship to include follow-up actions; Carol Chapman of Cuneiform Graphics did the layout of the papers in this volume; Babs Basson of Kagiso Publishers was the helpful and efficient publisher, along with essential input from others such as Irene Cornelissen; Charles Malan and Pieter Conradie of the Human Sciences Research Council gave pointers on lines of follow-up; Annemarie Ferns, Carel Breedt and Joseph Nhlapo of the SA Communication Service gave direction to communication planning; Piet Liebenberg, André Fourie and Victor Mhangwane of Business Against Crime were receptive to cooperation in implementation. And, as already mentioned, the list still grows.

Alewyn Burger
(Chairman, Organising Committee
South African representative of the IWC)

Other members serving on the Organising Committee at various times were:

Institute of World Concerns: Callie Swart, Kobus Swart, Abner Naanyane, Jurgens van Zyl and Chris Whiteley

National Peace Structures: Val Pauquet, Andries van Rensburg and Peter Batchelor

University of South Africa: Jan de Jongh van Arkel and Mandla Makhanya

National Plan for Family Life/Department of Welfare: Louise Erasmus, Claude Möller and Rita Verster

FAMSA (Family and Marriage Council of SA): Annette van Rensburg and Nelda van Zyl
SABTA (SA Black Taxi Association): Cyprian Lebese
SANCO (SA National Civics Organisation): Lechesa Tsenoli
UME (United Municipal Executive): Jimmy Sadie
Media adviser: Peet Simonis
Conference Planners: Cilla Taylor, Ammie Wissing and Alyson Lee-Cox.

Offices of the *Institute of World Concerns*

In South Africa:
 PO Box 17177
 Groenkloof
 0027

In the United Kingdom:
 Nettle Hill
 Brinklow Road
 Ansty
 Coventry CV7 9JL

In the United States of America:
 2215 East Michigan Avenue
 Lansing
 MI 48912

Keynote address:

The role of the family, church and school in fostering attitudes for peace and development

Bryn Jones

Covenant Ministries International; a Founding Director: Institute of World Concerns

Abstract

Reconstruction and development are essential for peace. In this process of peace-making we must reject trite answers and be aware of the high risks involved and the great commitment required.

Our concept of peace must include fellowship and the mutual bestowal of dignity and respect. Unity should refer to a harmonious diversity and not just tolerance of division or the assimilation of one culture by another. To end violence, the influences that give rise to aggressive acts must be removed, as violence is often a child of injustice. Substantial financial and human costs will be required to bring equality and justice for all in all relationships and systems.

The cradles of peace and development are the main institutions of our society. Government has to ensure welfare and justice for all and guard over the weak and poor. Economic policy is a key area affecting people most deeply, and should be judged by its effect on personal dignity and self-worth, not for a few but for all.

The family's strength is the foundation of society. Parental dignity must be preserved, and the economic system should strengthen and not exploit the family. The first influence on a child is the family, where attitudes of respect for authority, responsibility, decision and self-value are learnt.

The school must serve both the privileged and the poor, and teachers have a high vocation with tremendous influence in the most formative years. In education as employment, affirmative action should be wisely planned.

Society practises the art of living together through accepted patterns of social behaviour and beliefs. In a multi-cultural society it is important to bridge schisms and impregnate the social structure with love. For this, strong leadership and cooperation at every level are needed.

The church has played a prophetic role in the peace settlement, and now faces the new challenge of the transformation of society for positive peace. It must monitor the morality and emphasise the moral dimension in every policy consideration, support family structure and values, remind of the necessity of educating the whole person, and discourage domination by a minority or intimidation by a majority.

It is with a deep sense of challenge and responsibility that I join you at this conference.

The recent violent past of this nation sobers our vision of the future. The wounds are deep, the pains so personal and potent that they temper our contributions. Nevertheless, for us the pursuit of peace, reconstruction and development is essential, not optional. To fail to pursue these objectives is to fail those who have already died for them. A lasting peace requires us to face some harsh facts and ask ourselves the questions we would rather avoid. We must reject the trite answers and simplistic formulas which are the currency of shallow thinkers. The issue of fostering peace is a complex one and to be true peacemakers demands the deepest thinking, the highest risks and a commitment too great for those proffering instant solutions.

In this introduction, I would like to provide an essential context for thought and set the perimeters for dialogue.

In order to create a constructive dialogue, it is essential to define our use of such words as *peace, unity, violence* and even *justice* itself. Failure to speak with mutually understood words is to agree a price without determining the currency.

Peace

In speaking of *peace* I am not referring simply to the absence of conflict between peoples, but to the enjoyment of fellowship amongst peoples. Positive peace was not arrived at by the ending of apartheid, that was a stage on the journey to the acceptance of each other as equals. People were enabled to bestow dignity and respect on each other which is a prerequisite to achieving the integration of peoples which is the threshold of positive peace.

Unity

When I use the word *unity* it is not referring to tolerance of division but to a harmonious diversity. The unity we seek will not be brought about by the assimilation of one people by the other, or one culture by another. God forbid such a blandness born of blindness in the nation. Unity is the welcome creation of the integrated richness of our diversity. To maintain unity may at times require peripheral cultural concessions yet it never demands cultural compromise – that is the undermining of what is essential to a culture. Happily, unity is not the end of difference, only the end of discord.

Violence

When I speak of the end of *violence*, I am looking beyond the aggressive acts of individuals upon other members of society. I am looking to the end of all influences that give rise to violence, that nurture violence, that provoke violence.

We often condemn violence and call for its end without being willing to consider the fact that violence is often a child of injustice. To see violent conflicts give way to celebrations of peace, requires more than hope, faith or dialogue; it requires correct action to secure the necessary changes for peace. Violence is the last resort for those who will not lie down and die, who will not go away or become invisible. Violence is their reaction to society's dismissal of them as non-existent. They see violence as the only way to get what is their basic human right, namely access to resources by which they may live.

Many people see South Africa's recent violent past as totally negative, a tragedy for which its people have paid dearly. Others, like myself, believe that history will show that the tragic horror of these years was inevitable given the circumstances at the time, and was only engaged in as a last resort by those tired of interminably postponed promises of change. Thank God there came the moment when the voice of men, women and children crying out, "enough is enough, let us build our future in peace together" finally prevailed.

Justice

For peace to flourish we must establish *justice* in social and family relationships, as well as in the economic and educational systems. For too long the injustice of institutionalised inequality and the denial of human rights, have provided the nutrients which feed the tree of violence. Now the axe must be laid to the roots of that tree. The establishing of justice touches every individual, family, school, college, university, business and political party in the nation. Such is the nature of humanity that the principles of equality and justice for all members of society, irrespective of culture, race or religion, must be fully supported by the legal and judicial system. The demands for justice will not be met easily, as Dr. Martin Luther King Jnr. stated: "Justice so long deferred has accumulated interest and its cost for this society will be substantial in financial as well as human terms."[1]

Cradles of peace and development

I want to now address the main institutions of our society which protect peace while it is developing. Together they will establish foundations for the peaceful domestic and social life of the community.

Government is appointed by God for society as a whole. It has received Divine authority to secure the welfare and good of all people under its rule, to minister justice to the benefit of all. It should be especially vigilant to its guardianship of the weak and poor.

Perhaps at no point does a government affect people as easily and deeply as in its economic policy.

All economic policies and systems are to be judged by whether they take away personal dignity and self-worth, or whether they protect and reinforce those values. The economic system must be judged not by what it achieves *for the few*, but by what it does *for all.* To deny any basic right to earn a living, is to condemn them to hunger, misery, homelessness and poverty, the multiplying seed of institutionalised economic injustice. Economic policies that subjugate people to market forces, eventually destroys the social conscience which leads to unemployment being declared tolerable, and later, the economic gnomes will assert unemployment to be necessary in a modern economic system. Should this be accepted, then men and women will have become disposable items in a nightmare world ruled by the money market.

Peace demands change in the core values of our society. A change that reinstates honour and dignity to men and women. The government must set the pace by examining closely its economic policy.

For many the prospect of a just economic system is an impossible dream. But if we desire peace and development there must arise the hope of such and a people with determination to realise that hope. We must avoid ideological extremes, yet broaden the base of economic power. We must devise new structures for economic co-operation and partnership between government and the private sector, employers and employees, management and trade unions. It is vital that South Africa attracts foreign investment for its development. This is not easy in today's highly competitive international commercial, financial and technological network. But one fundamental principle must be held inviolate. While seeking international investment we must not allow the wealth and well-being of a minority to increase at the expense of the majority nor vice versa.

Every economic decision and policy must be judged not only by what it achieves for the upwardly mobile middle class, but how it effects the least in the weave of the social fabric of the nation. Failure of government in serving society will lead to government turning in on itself and simply serving those in positions of power. A situation all too common in many parts of Africa.

The family

The family is the basic unit of society, and as such we recognise that the stability and health of the family structure will directly influence the health of society as a whole. The strength of the family is the foundation of society itself. You cannot allow the disintegration of family life and expect society to remain unified.

For the family to be strong it is essential that parental dignity must be preserved, which means there must be sufficient finance to provide for their children. The economic system must strengthen the family, not exploit it.

The cradle of the family is where the learning processes of a child first emerge; the child learns at home before it learns at school. It is here that positive attitudes of respect for authority, responsibility in life, the power of decision, the value of one's self, are planted as seed by parents or grandparents. This deposit should then be reinforced at school.

School

Education policies must no longer serve the privileged while relegating the poor to second-class education. Second-class education today is third-class citizenship tomorrow.

To those who are teachers let me say yours is not simply a job, but a vocation. Next to the child's parent you are the greatest influence for good upon that child. Often the hours they spend with you in the classroom are more than those spent with a parent at home. What is more, your influence as role model and mentor is being brought to bear on them during the most impressionable and formative years or their lives. They are at the age when they question established values, attitudes, society, government, even life itself. Do not treat your role lightly. You have the opportunity to instill and strengthen a value system and attitude that will be a lasting investment for good in the person. In doing this you will have played a major part in securing a better future for the child, and ultimately the nation as a whole.

In the context of South Africa it is essential that where the consequences of past discriminations are affecting the present, then the government has the obligation to take positive practical steps to overcome this legacy of injustice. In education as employment, there is a case for wisely planned affirmative action programmes.

Society

By society we mean that grouping or system of accepted forms of social behaviour and belief that hold people together by common consent. Examples of this are language, customs, political and community groups. These are means by which individuals are held in a free but cohesive framework for functioning together. The concept of society emphasises the interaction of individuals in their relationship together. As Reinhold Niebuhr stated, society is "the art of living together".

There is a native American Indian saying with respect to the family, and the child's welfare: "It takes a village to rear a child." This highlights everyone's responsibility to be socially interdependent. It demands supportive, interactive relationship between peoples.

In a nation formerly so divided, to achieve cohesion in society is a major challenge on every level. The socio-historical abuse and divides of the past may be erased from the constitutional framework, but to erase them from the mind and soul of individuals is far more difficult.

Society's schisms and complexities must first be healed and bridged in order for them to play their proper roles in the securing of peace for all. The structure of social relations must be impregnated with love for God and fellow man.

This challenge and privilege are especially important in a multi-cultural pluralistic society. The dangers and pitfalls we face in pursuit of this ideal are many. Failure to negotiate the dangerous terrain could lead again to an eruption of violence; however, we will not fail to advance for fear. Our progress to the hoped-for peace will be with a faith sufficient for the journey.

Individuals and groups at every level of social life must seek to work together to promote an atmosphere conducive to the evolution of peace and prosperity for all peoples. Society, therefore, will need a strong voice of leadership so that it may not falter or deviate from the hoped-for goal, and that brings me to the final cradle of peace: the church.

The Church

No one can over-estimate the role the church has already played in helping secure the peace settlement to date. There has come from within the church a strong prophetic voice in a political and social wilderness. It has cried out loudly on behalf of the oppressed. It has inspired men and women of strong character and prophetic insight. Some of these people suffered greatly, some were tortured, some have even died, their blood continues to cry out for peace with justice. We are humbled by the memory and knowledge of their deeds and we will remain ever grateful. However, let me say to the church there is now a new and probably greater challenge facing you. A negotiated settlement has been reached, but positive peace is yet to be gained and established. The church must raise its voice again to lead in the prophetic task of the transformation of society in securing a positive peace for the future of the nation.

* It is necessary for the church to judge the morality of government policy to protect and to assure progress for the poor, the lost, the traumatised, and those too weak to stand alone.

* It is necessary for the church to emphasise the moral dimension in every policy consideration.

* It is necessary for the church to clearly define and support the family structure and the values which undergird it.

* It is for the church to remind the government of the necessity of educating the whole person, rather than simply emphasising a curriculum suited for the development of the intellect alone.

* It is for the church to remind the nation that in order for positive peace to be achieved there must never be a domination of the majority by the minority, nor an intimidation of the minority by the majority.

* * * * * * * * * * * * * * *

My appeal to you as fellow delegates is: Let us not run from debating these issues, nor side-step the difficulties by retreating to the safety zones of the intransigent mind.

* Let us risk being wrong, if it leads to finding what is right.
* Let us risk the pain of change if it will lead to peace.
* Let us risk confrontation if it opens up our reasoning.
* Let this generation risk hurt in loving again if it will secure the foundation for peace, for future generations.

Ladies and gentlemen, fellow delegates, the tree of peace is filled with the sap of blood; it must be nurtured well for if mistreated it will bleed again.

As the American poet Maya Angelou said,

"History, despite its wrenching pain,
Cannot be unlived, but if faced
With courage, need not be lived again." [2]

Peace: Shalom: Khotso: Vrede: Ukuthula.

References

1. J.M. Washington. (Ed.) 1986. *A Testament of Hope, the essential writings of Martin Luther King, Jr.* San Francisco: Harper & Row, Publishers.
2. *On the Pulse of Morning:* Inauguration poem for President Clinton, USA.

The calamity of the social sciences and the problem of evil

Prof. Victor Nell

Health Psychology Research Unit, Unisa;
Centre for Peace Action, Eldorado Park

Abstract

The social sciences, and especially scientific psychology, are modernistic products that cannot acknowledge or come to grips with the immanence of evil at every level of human behaviour – interpersonally, in the struggle for political power, and in the conduct of nations.

The normative view of human affairs is still that of the Enlightenment – that humanity is perfectible, and that this perfection will inevitably be attained through the triumph of reason. Media culture reinforces these modernistic assumptions by presenting a just world in which the right and the good always triumph, and in which the use of violence is either morally justified or soon punished. These Enlightenment convictions hold sway despite the abundant evidence of evil triumphant all over the world. As a result, evil deeds are incomprehensible (and therefore of little interest to social scientists) unless they are presented within a social Darwinist frame as "primitive" (Rwanda, Angola or East Timor) or marginalised as the work of inhuman monsters (Auschwitz, the Gulags).

The social sciences must therefore take account of the evolutionary and historical record and develop an alternative to this modernistic construction of human nature which rejects the dismissal of evil, acknowledges its immanence, and in this light comes to grips not with the "science" of human behaviour, but its reality.

There are two trains of thought I would like to follow with you this morning. The first is the nature of evil, its immanence, its ever-present and consuming reality in the human heart. The second is the problem of differing personal values, and how deeply a secular individual like me can link with deeply believing people like you. If, because of our differing beliefs, we cannot talk to one another at both an intellectual level (at which we like to believe that policy and plans are made) and an emotional level, listening to our hearts and bellies as well as our heads (the level at which policy is really made) we will neutralise rather than reinforce one another, with the religious community pulling one way, and the secular majority ignoring or ridiculing them.

The calamity of the social sciences

One looks in vain to the social sciences for guidance on the conduct of human affairs. One of the reasons is their deliberate exclusion of the emotions from their field of study. This is a strange state of affairs.

If psychology is the science of behaviour, it seems self-evident that it must study the emotions at least as closely as the operations of intellect. The events that most deeply affect the lives of most people on this planet arise from the belly, not the brain. Wars, famines and the systematic torture of millions of people (euphemistically called "human rights abuses") have their origin in the greed and power lust of politicians, not their rationality; ordinary men and women assault one another and their children in moments of passion, not thoughtfulness; the world's two most lucrative businesses, the entertainment industry and the arms industry, feed on the need men have – men more than women – to mutilate and kill.

Yet in late 20th century psychology and the other social sciences, emotion and the related problem of evil are out of fashion. Psychologists can spend an entire professional life without paying more than passing attention to "affectivity", a sanitary term behind which the stench of the passions, the smell of blood and of excrement, can be hidden. Cognitive psychology supports a large academic industry, but there is no journal on evil.

I was reflecting on the emotionlessness of the social sciences at the opening of this conference last night. I was touched and moved by Alewyn Burger's opening prayer, by the messages of support from the Institute of World Concerns and the National Peace Committee, in a way that I have never been touched at any of the dozens of psychological conferences I have attended. There is a heart here, and only a head there.

The immanence of evil

Let us now turn back to the first of the two threads, the immanence of evil. As a result, I am going to be talking today about terrible things, and it would be wrong to apologise for doing so. It is shocking but necessary to acknowledge the immanence of evil as a living presence in each of us, even though modern science denies this reality.

The social sciences are bankrupt in the face of evil. One way of bringing this issue to a focus is by considering what happened to little James Bulger, who was abducted from a shopping centre in England in February last year. The abductors were Robert Thompson, who was referred to throughout the trial as Child A, and Jon Venables, Child B. The body of James, a two-year-old baby, was discovered on Sunday, February 14. He had been stripped of his trousers and underpants, and then beaten to death with bricks, an iron bar, fists and feet. The imprint of Child A's shoe was found on his face. Child B told the investigators that they had beaten James with bricks, but he just kept getting back up. This angered Child A, who screamed at him, "Stay down, you stupid divvy!" "He probably did it for fun", continued Child B, "he was laughing his head off." The dead or dying child, with blood inside his mouth and wounded genitals, was then tossed onto the railway line.

In finding the boys guilty, Mr Justice Morland called the murder "cunning and wicked . . . an act of unparalleled evil". *The Star* ran the verdict on its front page on November 26 last year, under the headline, "Why? Ask Stunned Britons?" That was also the headline in the *New York Times* on the same day: "After Murder, Britain Asks Why?"

Why indeed? What explanatory hypotheses for this terrible deed, the deliberate, repetitive torture of a baby over a period of hours by two ten-year-old children, can be offered?

Why is an explanation important?

Violence and the problem of evil

South Africa is the most violent country in the world. Its male homicide rate is 56/100 000 p.a., nearly 3 times higher than St. Lucia (22,6/100 000), the next most violent country listed by the World Health Organisation. Violence prevention is therefore a high priority of the new South African government, to which the UNISA Health Psychology Unit is contributing through the violence prevention programmes of its affiliated Centre for Peace Action in the black suburbs south of Johannesburg created by the Group Areas Act (Eldorado Park, Chiawelo and Lenasia).

Eldorado Park, a so-called Coloured area, contributes more violence to the Johannesburg total than any other except Hillbrow. The personal injury rate among young coloured men is horrendous, far in excess of that for any other ethnic group. Epidemiological studies carried out by the Health Psychology Unit at public and private hospitals in the Johannesburg magisterial district show that 1 800 Coloured men aged between 18 and 24 out of every 100 000 present each year at hospitals for treatment arising from physical trauma; most of the trauma in this age group is caused by interpersonal violence. This figure of 1,8% far exceeds any other available in the statistical database of the World Health Organisation, and this represents only the tip of the iceberg, since most cases of domestic or "minor" violence would not present at hospitals.

Violence prevention requires an understanding of the fundamental intrapsychic predisposers to political, criminal and purely wanton violence; this in turn requires the development of a psychology of evil with a taxonomy of evil acts and a specification of the phenomenological and physiological reward systems that operate in each of its domains.

There is very little social science research on evil. In the PsycLit database of 398 000 journal articles from 1987 to mid-1994, only 189 titles or abstracts contain the word "evil"; this is 0,06% of the total. The psychodynamic approaches to evil have been marginalised by modern psychology; the pioneering empirical work on obedience to authority by Stanley Milgram in 1974 – the famous "Eichmann experiment" – and the wave of research on violence and the brain that began in the 1950s, and dried up 20 years later, were inconclusive. None of this work has generated focused and systematic study of the deliberate, often joyous infliction of suffering on other living creatures.

Modernism and original sin

All the currently available explanations for the murder of James Bulger can be reduced to two. One is unfashionable, because on religious or secular grounds it acknowledges the reality and power of evil, saying that what is horrifying about these children is their normality.

The other is scientific and modern. The essence of modernism is the belief of the 18th century European Enlightenment that human nature is perfectible, and that this perfection will inevitably be obtained through the light of reason, through which man understands the universe and improves his own condition. The Enlightenment's most enduring legacy is the belief that human history is a record of general progress. Two centuries on, us children of the Enlightenment continue passionately to believe in progress.

There is no room in this system for Child A and Child B. If they belong to the human race, modernism is wrong, and history cannot be a record of general progress. If humanity is perfecting itself, these terrible children must be dehumanised. And this is exactly what the world's press, in defence of the principle of progress, proceeded to do. British tabloids branded the boys "evil demons" (*The Star*, November 26). Newsweek ran a story under the headline, "What kind of child would kill a child?" and Maclean's Magazine entitled its story, "Beyond the edge of evil": a later Maclean's story was headlined, "Children of a monster society".

Popular consciousness has no answer to the insistent question of Why? By monsterising the children, or by suggesting, as the judge and many politicians did, that sex-and-violence videos – "video nasties" – had given rise to the children's brutality, a quick and easy answer to the question is found, namely that the children are not fully human, and that their behaviour is not therefore a threat to the social belief system.

But the social sciences do no better than the mass media in giving an explanation. One of the most thoughtful articles on the case was written by Elizabeth Newsom, Professor of Developmental Psychology at the University of Nottingham (*The Psychologist*, 1994, pp. 272-276). She correctly resists trivialising the incident as the work of "evil freaks," but can offer no explanation beyond a link with media violence.

This is not an adequate explanation. Part of the problem is that there is almost no social science research on the psychology of evil.

Seymour Sarason, the great American community psychologist, gives part of the explanation of this wilful blindness. He writes that psychology "serves the social order because it has been socialised into the social order" and therefore cannot "take distance from it" (*Psychology Misdirected*, 1981, p.x). This is why psychologists (and other social scientists) struggle to comprehend a society "that is in them or in those people whom they seek to help" (p.112). This is a pregnant phrase, "the society that is in them": For the fish, there is no water. It is precisely the most fundamental and universally accepted beliefs of one's society that become background rather than foreground, and as a result escape investigation. Optimism has driven the study of evil underground.

Impelled by irresistible cultural and commercial forces, the media reinforce these modernistic assumptions. James Bond and Enid Blyton's Little Noddy do not have much in common except that, as media creatures, both inhabit a just world in which the right and the good always triumph, and in which the use of violence by Bond or Mr Plod is morally justified, and violence against them soon punished. The abundant evidence of evil triumphant all over the world is neutralised by portraying it either as the work of inhuman monsters (Auschwitz, the Gulags) or, when it occurs in the developing world, by presenting it within a social Darwinist frame as "primitive" (Rwanda, East Timor or the Congo).

The unfashionable explanation is to acknowledge that the capacity to do terrible things is deeply rooted in human nature. As Hannah Arendt says of Eichmann, what is terrifying about Child A and Child B is their normality. The Catholic view of the darkness of the human heart is the doctrine of original sin, "a hereditary and universal moral defect that makes human beings incapable . . . even of achieving basic human decency". When Noah sacrificed to God after the flood had subsided, "the Lord said in his heart, I will not again curse the ground any more for man's sake; for the imagination of man's heart is evil from his youth" (Genesis 8:21). Only God's redemptive grace can lift an individual human being from this fallen state. Murderers and torturers are not monsters, but profoundly human; they have not been touched by grace.

Laughing crowds

But there is no persuasive secular-scientific theory to account for human evil. What light would an "archaeology of behaviour" cast on this problem? What would an examination of the behavioural sediments in human history tell us about normative human nature?

A 4th century mosaic now in the Villa Borghese in Rome shows a contest between gladiators in the Roman arena. The *Retiarii*, lightly armed with a net and dagger in one hand, and a trident in the other, are shown getting the better of the Samnites, heavily armed with a visor, oblong shield and short sword. The arena was enormously wasteful of human and animal lives, and from the time of Julius Caesar until the 2nd century, the games became more and more extravagant. The Emperor Trajan (98-117 AD) celebrated his victories in Dacia with an entertainment that lasted four months in which 10 000 wild animals imported from Africa and the Asian empire, and 10 000 gladiators, were sent to the arena. None of the animals and very few of the gladiators survived. A favoured type of contest was the *Munus sine missione*, a tournament from which no-one was allowed to emerge alive.

These scenes of brutal murder, in which reluctant gladiators were goaded with red-hot irons and the sand of the arena clotted with blood, were enormously popular. The terrible thing, more terrible than the murder, is the delight these spectacles gave the spectators, who were moved to a frenzy of excitement and sexual arousal. The arena was frequented by Rome's prostitutes.

Spectacles of pain and death were a fixed part of medieval life, and torture was not unique to the Inquisition. There was nothing the Inquisition did that was not commonplace in the procedures of ordinary criminal justice. The power of a sovereign was expressed through the torture inflicted on the body of the condemned criminal, and the torment was calculated to be infinitely greater than the crime that had been committed. The route taken by the procession to the gallows was planned so as to involve the whole of the urban fabric in the demonstration of the sovereign's awful power with maximum public involvement. Bound hand and foot, the condemned man or woman was drawn to the gallows on the executioner's cart, and his flesh was torn with red-hot tongs during this endless journey. The execution was even more frightful than these preliminary torments. Great crowds followed the executioner's wagon, and gathered at the place of execution. As in the arena, death was entertainment.

These gruesome processions attended by laughing crowds continued into modern times. Goya's caption to an illustration in the *Caprichos*, a series of etchings published in 1799, reads, "There was no cure. They had made up their minds to kill this good woman. After judgement was pronounced, she was dragged through the streets in triumph . . ." In the *Disasters of War*, Goya recorded the atrocities committed by both sides in the Peninsular War in which Napoleon led his armies into Spain. One of these shows a man being hung from a tree. The tree is too low for the body to fall, so the soldiers pull against the noose, strangling him gradually. The soldier on the left is grinning.

Evil in hiding

In passing judgement on the Roman arena and medieval executions from the vantage point of what appears to us to be a morally superior civilisation, we need to remember that what separates us from the Romans is no more than secrecy and concealment. We send our sons to war to be trained how to kill a man face to face in unarmed combat – crush the Adam's apple, snap the cervical spine – or with rifle butts and bayonets, and how to kill scientifically from a great distance with laser-guided bombs and airburst explosions that suck the lungs out through the mouth, or by booby traps that mutilate but do not kill: a wounded soldier is a greater drain on the enemy's resources than a dead one. The pleasure of killing is hidden behind masks of righteousness: national security, the defence of freedom; the use of violence and torture becomes morally righteous. In *Dusklands*, John Coetzee writes: "The gun is our mediator with the world and therefore our saviour . . . The gun saves us from the fear that all life is within us. It does so by laying at our feet all the evidence we need of a dying and therefore a living world."

Evil cannot be "dehumanised" or driven into hiding. Its reality must be acknowledged, and it must become a mainstream research topic in the social sciences. Video nasties don't come out of the minds of solitary perverts:

they are a symbolic expression of the values we live by. The most profound cultural disease is the worship of pseudo-masculinity that places the highest value on aggression, domination and winning at all costs in the classroom, in the business world, in politics and in war.

Values are the most fundamental determinants of behaviour. The only barrier that can be built against the darkness of the human heart is the development of values from early childhood, nurtured and reinforced until adulthood, that are profoundly respectful of all life, animal and human, and horrified by suffering.

Like grace, values can redeem human nature.

Empowering the church for economic development

Congressman Walter Tucker III
US House of Representatives

Abstract

For African-Americans, the "church" has long been a place of refuge, comfort, solace and guidance in an often hostile and violent country. In 1992 the city of Los Angeles erupted into the bloodiest and costliest rebellion in United States history. Not surprisingly, commentators and pundits were quick to point out what members of the African-American community had already known: The rebellion stemmed from the lack of economic and social justice in our community.

Immediately after the rebellion, religious leaders throughout the city and country began to re-evaluate the role of the church in securing social justice in our communities. What these ministers quickly came to realise was that, without economic clout and to some exent economic autonomy, social justice could not and would not be guaranteed. For many churches throughout the country this was not a new revelation. Indeed some of these churches had long ago made a commitment of church resources to economic empowerment within their communities. The city-wide rebellion led to a new-found unity of purpose: the economic empowerment of all African-American communities.

For many people, both inside and outside the community, the rebellion was symbolic of this injustice. In Los Angeles county – where 1 308 255 people live in poverty; where 496 940 of those in poverty are children; where 40% of all African-American youth between the ages of 16 and 25 are unemployed; where the parents of these youths are unemployed to the tune of 18%; where the lack of ownership in local businesses and the inability of members of our community to access capital through the insidious practice of "redlining" exists – it is certainly conceivable that the resentment and hopelessness bred by these factors led to the rebellion.

With the foregoing statistics clearly on each of their minds the Congressional Black Caucus of the United States House of Representatives recently held its 24th Annual Legislative Conference in Washington, D.C. During this conference I, along with Congressmen Floyd Flake (D-New York), and Albert Wynn (D-Maryland), convened both a workshop and Congressional Hearing to see if we could bring together as many forces as possible for the purpose of "Economic Empowerment" in the African-American community.

Many of the speakers spoke of forging new partnerships, using public and private sources, including the church, as resources of funding to spur economic empowerment and development in the African-American community. If African-

Americans are to realise the promise of liberty and justice promised to all Americans, the church, the government, private and public financial institutions, individuals and communities must all do their part. We must forge these new partnerships!

Thank you for this opportunity to discuss a few ideas about empowering the church for economic development. This universal concept is currently at work in several communities in the United States. My objective today is to share with you a few ideas about how the South African church, in concert with the federal government, should secure for her people economic and social justice.

In a recent editorial, I offered the following opinion: "The strongest moral force in the lives of most people is the church". For African-Americans in particular, the church has been a place of refuge, comfort, solace and guidance in an often hostile and violent country.

A few years ago the city of Los Angeles experienced the costliest rebellion in United States history. Not surprisingly, commentators and pundits were quick to point out what members of the African-American community had already known. The rebellion "stemmed from a lack of economic and social justice in the African-American community."

According to Bartley L. McSwine, as early as the 19th century Alex De Tocqueville, writing after his visit to America from France, and Gunnar Myrdal, writing after his visit from Sweden, spoke of similar contradictions in America between rich and poor, black and white. Echoing W.E.B. Dubois who said in 1906 that the problem of the 20th century was the problem of the colour line, Myrdal concluded in 1944 that this problem of race was a major American dilemma that, if not dealt with, would tear this country apart. The promise of white society as reflected in the U.S. Constitution, the Pledge of Allegiance, the Gettysburg Address and the general ethos of equality as promoted by these documents, contrasted sharply with the reality of poverty and prejudice as practised on a daily basis, he said. The recent uprising in Los Angeles and other major cities across this country are a manifestation of these contradictions in the late 20th century American empire.[1]

For many people, both inside and outside the community, the rebellion was symbolic of this injustice. In Los Angeles county where 1 308 255 persons live in poverty; where 40% of all African-American youth between the ages of 16 and 25 are unemployed; where the parents of these youths are unemployed to the tune of 18%; where the lack of ownership in local businesses and the inability of members of our community to access capital through the insidious practice of "redlining"; it is conceivable that the resentment and hopelessness bred by these factors led to the rebellion.

After four hundred or more years of our blood, sweat and tears, the African-American still finds that he is an unwanted stranger in the home he helped to build. While my fathers and forefathers did not immigrate to America in the same way other émigrés did, our contributions were and are no less significant and deserving of a fair share in the fruits of the Gross National Product (GNP) pie.

Immediately after the rebellion, religious leaders throughout the city and the country began to re-evaluate the role of the "church" in securing social justice in our community. What these religious leaders found was that the more economic autonomy there was in the community the more economic and social justice you would find.

While this revelation was not new to our community and indeed congregations of African-American churches throughout the country had long ago made a commitment of church resources to empowering the communities they served; the newly found unity of purpose by these churches provided the impetus for many more churches to go forward with the challenge of assisting in economic empowerment. In essence, these congregations and their respective ministers, began to understand the need for the church to refocus its attention on the critical needs of the individual and the whole community rather than on just the spiritual or religious needs.

Africans on the continent and Africans throughout the diaspora are continually polled on the importance and influence of the church in their everyday lives. I stand today convinced of the church's ability to change the economic well-being of our community. On economic empowerment through the church, Eric Lincoln writes, "the black church knows the power of a holistic commitment by *experience*, for it was born of a vast schedule of needs that a nation committed to slavery could not, or would not address. Those needs were spiritual in the first instance, of course, but they also were physical, social, psychological, and economic. They were the same needs we recognise today as necessary to a reasonably dignified human experience."[2]

Recently, the Congressional Black Caucus of the United States House of Representatives convened its 24th Annual Legislative Conference in Washington, D.C. Thousands of Africans from throughout the diaspora converged on the United States Capitol to talk about and offer solutions to some of the problems facing African-Americans.

During this conference I, along with Congressmen Flake (D-NY) and Wynn (D-MD) convened a workshop and official "hearing" to see if we could bring together public, private and government resources for the purpose of "economic empowerment" in the African-American community.

Ministers, Clinton Administration officials, private and church-based financial institutions, and representatives from throughout the country offered testimony on the problems facing our communities as well as the solutions some of them have implemented to confront the growing problem of economic deterioration in our communities.

Representatives from religious-based financial institutions spoke of the need to invest in community development credit unions dedicated to economic empowerment in the local communities. These representatives spoke of how church people are themselves based in a community which can put its energy and resources behind an economic justice project and this means that they can be effective participants in the process of community renewal. These representatives stressed that if directed toward areas of need, the financial resources of religious communities could make a significant difference in economic development. Many of these congregations are in areas in which economic development is severely hampered by the lack of available capital for business ventures. They further emphasised the tremendous impact the religious community could have by placing their investment capital into their own Federally insured financial institution where a significant percentage of its funds could be devoted to economic development in their region. The effect will be that churches themselves will actually be creating jobs in high unemployment areas.

In his farewell address as president of the Progressive National Baptist Convention, Dr. Charles G. Adams stated that: "The African-American Church is all that African-Americans own, control and lead. It sits in the middle of the dark and difficult ghetto. Everybody in the ghetto does not belong to the Church but the church belongs to everybody in the ghetto... Let us use it to encourage African-Americans to be partners, movers and shakers in the vast undeveloped vistas of economic possibility."

Administration officials from the Department of Housing and Urban Development spoke of their commitment to "put people first", the campaign promise of candidate Bill Clinton when running for the presidency. These representatives spoke of helping to make Urban and Rural Public Housing a source of pride to communities by encouraging resident participation in its management, downsizing large developments, restoring deteriorated buildings, offering residents a choice to move to low-poverty areas, giving residents incentives to work and lift themselves economically, and ensuring that these developments become safe, healthy, and attractive places to live and raise children. They also spoke of expanding urban and rural housing opportunities for low-income people through partnerships with state and local governments, private developers and lending institutions, and non-profit agencies, and reestablishing the Federal Housing Administration as an active support for creative metropolitan-wide housing and urban development initiatives; of further opening urban and rural housing markets to minorities through vigorous efforts to enforce fair housing laws. And finally, these representatives spoke of empowering urban and rural communities by supporting local efforts to transform neighborhoods, by reinvigorating economic development programs and creating new opportunities for people and businesses, and by supporting community-based organisations including the church.

In closing let me say, economic empowerment in and of itself should not be the focus, but the manifestation of a vision, focusing on helping the individual in the community, helping the institutions within the community and having as the effect … the empowering of the community!

This is a positive vision and it is time. But it will not be easy. Easy is fast. Easy is quick. Easy is fun. And easy is often an illusion. The right way to do something is based on truth and truth doesn't come easy. So as we deal with empowerment we're really talking about collaboration … forging partnerships!

For the people of South Africa, I urge you not to rush off to duplicate someone else's success. Think of your history, your institutions, and your communities and develop within this context methods that are uniquely right for South Africa and her people.

References

1. McSwine, Bartley L. 1993 "Why L.A. Happened". *L.A. 1992: Race, Class and Spiritual Poverty in the American Empire.* Third World Press.
2. Lincoln, Eric. *Economic Empowerment through the Church.*

Notes

Lessons on civic society from elsewhere:
The relevance of the social fabric to industrial activity, democracy and development

RSK (Bob) Tucker

Leader of Nedcor-Old Mutual scenario study

Abstract

Studies of developments over the last decades in Italy and in the previous century in the USA illustrate that the structure of society plays an important role in determining both the level of commercial and industrial activity and the effectiveness of democratic government.

The structure that facilitates economic activity and good government and empowers individuals is one that manifests 'horizontal' relationships. This means that many associations are formed in which people together pursue the objects of their common desires, reflecting their norms and values.

The opposite is a 'vertical' structure, in which individuals rely on authorities and institutions above them, which leads to patronage, dependency and inefficiency.

It is these structures, rather than genetic or racial difference, that are relevant in determining the course of development.

In South Africa, the primary problem regarding development is not contrasts in wealth or education, but the fact that we have one community functioning within a formal institutional fabric, in cultural affinity with it and hence 'empowered', and another community 'dependent' on that fabric, not in cultural affinity with it and hence not empowered.

Education on its own is not enough. Capacity building should be concerned with the institutional fabric, otherwise the prospects are bad for sustainable development, as well as for local government and industrial activity.

The required institutional fabric and civil society can be developed only at the grass-roots level, not by government (which represents the vertical type of relationships), nor by business (which builds on this fabric but tends to erode it).

The ethic that undergirded the value system when American development took off, was one of thrift and mutual support, leading to mutual respect, self-reliance and trust, which fed the horizontal structure of society.

In a competitive, materialistic society, democracy will not work and the community will be poor. If life is understood to be only part of the divine purpose and love is practised, the horizontal structures ensue from which wealth is generated. Then our needs are satisfied and we live in harmony and prosperity.

Thus commerce, industry, democracy and the institutional fabric are not the cause of prosperity, only symptoms of living in accord with God's command!

23

Between 1970 and 1990 the Italian government transferred approximately seventy per cent of the national expenditure budget from the central government to the local and regional governments. The local authorities in the North used the available funds very efficiently, and the communities in that region prospered. Others, predominantly in the South, used the funds ineffectively, and it seems as though the Mafia was the primary beneficiary of what was spent, while the local communities concerned continued to suffer relative to their Northern neighbours.

Most of us would probably attribute the good performance in the North to the fact that it is industrialised whereas the South is not, but tends rather to be dominated by the Mafia. However, very careful research over a period of twenty years has conclusively proved that industrialisation in the North is a consequence of precisely the same set of circumstances which tend to result in good government, and not that industrialisation in itself causes good government. Likewise the presence of Mafia activities is not the cause of ineffective government in the South, but a consequence of the same set of circumstances which tend to result in ineffective government there. Nor incidentally can good performance be attributed to stable government, some of the best performing authorities having suffered the highest level of volatility in that notoriously volatile country.

In fact the factor which so radically determines the type of government different communities will enjoy or suffer and the level of industrial activity in their area, is the structure of their society. The only really certain indicator of the potential effectiveness of government or level of industrial activity is the number of clubs, social organisations, unions and suchlike in the community – in other words the condition of the institutional fabric.

This institutional fabric is, itself, merely the manifestation of HORIZONTAL relationship structures within the community. Self-reliance, mutual trust, respect and co-operation between people at the grass-roots level results in societal structures and arrangements which facilitate economic activity and good government and "empower" the individual. This type of societal structure must be distinguished from one which is VERTICAL and in which the individuals rely not so much on each other but on "authorities" and "institutions" above them. Far from facilitating economic activity and good government and "empowering" the individual, this type of arrangement results in patronage, dependency and inefficiency.

Interestingly this finding coincides exactly with the observation of the French philosopher Alexis de Tocqueville when he visited the United States of America in the middle of the nineteenth century.

"Americans of all ages, all stations in life, and all types of disposition are forever forming associations. There are not only commercial and industrial associations in which all take part, but others of a thousand different types – religious, moral, serious, futile, very general and very limited, immensely large and very minute ... Thus the most democratic country in the world now is that in which men have in our time carried to the highest perfection the art of pursuing in common the objects of common desires and have applied this new technique to the greatest number of purposes."

It was the norms and values of the new American civil society embodied in their social practices and structures which enabled millions of illiterate and unskilled immigrants to overcome the enormous disadvantages with which they arrived there, and to apply effectively their innate energy and resourcefulness to their own and the nation's advantage. In fact in this sense education was more a "symptom" of development rather than the "cause".

It is noteworthy that both these foreign examples completely refute the relevance of any genetic or racial difference in the communities concerned. It is also interesting and of concern that business is one of the primary beneficiaries of those societal values and structures, in that it builds on them and utilises the networks within the community to expand business. Yet if conducted in the "Fordist" industrial fashion, business is then very destructive of precisely the values and structures on which it was established.

The South African dilemma, therefore, is not so much the fact that some people enjoy great wealth and others none, nor that some people have two or three houses and others none, nor even that some people have a university education and others none. The real issue is that on the one hand there is a predominantly white community which functions within a formal institutional fabric with which they are in cultural affinity, and consequently "empowered". On the other hand there is a predominantly black community which has become "dependent" on that same formal institutional fabric, but is neither in cultural affinity with it nor "empowered" by it.

When we talk of "capacity building" it is really the institutional fabric with which we should be concerned. Education on its own is not enough, and development agencies which either ignore this or perceive "process" to be a necessary evil to get the co-operation of the "target" community, are missing the point. It is not just that there will be no sustainable development without institution building, but also that the prognosis for devolution of power, local government, and industrial activity are not good as long as the institutional fabric at grass-roots level remains weak, undeveloped and unreflective of the norms and values of the people in those communities.

Government and business can't do the work of developing the institutional fabric and civil society. That process can only take place at grass-roots level and government is in precisely the vertical type relationship which is the problem in the first place. Business, on the other hand, which is built on this fabric then tends to erode it.

It is not without significance that at the time American development took off in the middle of the nineteenth century, the "Puritan Ethic" was dominant in the country, and undergirded the value system at the time. Fundamental to that ethic were values of thrift and mutual support. It was therefore nor surprising that in a community with such a value system, an ambience of mutual respect, self-reliance and trust would prevail. This naturally resulted in a very horizontal structure to the society and consequently an environment in which people combined together in a whole range of different institutions, as described by de Tocqueville. The consequences as described by him was the sort of structure which prevails in the North of Italy, and which is conducive not only to the emergence of good working democracy, but also to the establishment of industry and commerce, and most importantly to the "enrichment" of the communities in question.

Here we perhaps begin to see the manifestation of God's eternal promise – that He will satisfy all our needs. In a very competitive survivalistic society, such as the one in which we live – where the prevailing belief is that we are the consequence of an atomic accident, that we are only here for 70 short years, that our best chance is to make the most of that short life because there is nothing after, and where we are only likely to prosper because others fail – there will be anything but the sort of environment in which society functions effectively, and so wealth will not be generated, democracy will not work and the community will be poor.

But where we live out the command to love our neighbour, where our life here is understood to be only part of the Divine purpose, where trust and mutual respect abound and labour is understood to be a primary resource to be maximised and not a cost of production to be minimised, then the horizontal structure necessary for the generation of real and sustainable wealth will be manifest at all levels, from the football and bird-watching clubs to the national government and the large financial institutions.

And so we will, in our everyday lives, see God's divine purpose fulfilled, all our needs satisfied, and we will live in harmony and prosperity together.

But we need to understand that living our lives in accord with God's command is the cause of the prosperity enjoyed in many communities around the world, and that the commerce, industry, working democracy, and rich institutional fabric which are found in such communities are symptoms of building on the rock. Commerce, industry, democracy and institutional fabric are neither the rock nor the cause of the prosperity.

It is therefore imperative that everyone who is concerned about sustainable development and future prosperity for all the people of this country should be giving attention to the values and forces which prevail in our society and which are tending to erode rather than underpin the horizontal structures and institutional fabric on which future prosperity will be dependent.

Notes

Women's and the family's contribution to peace and development

Ms Jessie Duarte
MEC for Safety and Security, Gauteng

Paper not received.

In view of Ms Duarte's critical involvement in South Africa's political scene during this time, the organisers accepted that the publication of the proceedings would have to continue without her important contribution.

Notes

Improving family life to curb youth violence

Jerome R. Nance

Co-convenor: St. Louis Consortium for
African-American Male Survival, USA

Abstract

The question of why many communities, cities, and nations experience costly and damaging youth violence is a complex one. There have been numerous studies investigating the nature and scope of this problem, identifying reasons for its existence, determining the rate of its growth, and suggesting measures to be taken to lessen its impact on its victims effectively. Even though vast differences of opinion exist among the professionals and academicians as to the primary risk factors causing this threat to peace and development, there is widespread agreement among the experts that in order to reduce violence risk factors and keep young people from becoming involved in violence and crime, family involvement is essential, beginning at the earliest possible point in time; for without the support of functional and involved families, all community efforts to bring solution to this problem fall short of their goals.

The intention of this paper is to:

* *point out the critical importance of improving family life to curb youth violence, and*

* *suggest ideas for action which families can consider as they attempt to foster attitudes which enhance peace, development and reconstruction.*

Introduction

The environment in which most American families live their lives is so constantly plagued by the threat and/or experience of youth violence, that it is safe to conclude that youth violence significantly diminishes the quality of life in the United States. Poll results point to the fact that youth violence touches Americans of all geographic areas and racial and ethnic groups. An opinion survey of 758 youths in the 10 to 17 age group was conducted in 1993 by Newsweek Magazine and the Center for Disease Control and Prevention to measure the extent of public anxiety about the threat of violence to children. It pointed out that fear of violence topped the list of worries for children and parents alike, with 56 percent of the youths and 73 percent of their parents saying they worry about violent crime against a family member.[1]

In another study by Harvard University, 2 508 elementary, middle, and high school students around the country were polled. Roughly the same percentages of inner-city and suburban students said they had been shot at, had been seriously threatened with a gun, or had fired a gun at someone else. Asked to estimate their chances of being killed by a gun before reaching old age, 54 percent of black students, 30 percent of white students, 41 percent of Latino students, and 43 percent of Asian students answered "somewhat likely" or "very likely". The definition of youth violence has expanded from the earlier boundaries of disorderly conduct and fist fights. Today's statistics measure the incidence of such crimes as assault and battery, robbery, car-jacking, and homicide. Many youths have become involved in gang activities which promote extreme anti-social behavior resulting in the destruction of property and loss of life. Suicide, drug abuse, and other self-destructive activity also contribute to youth violence accounting.

Effects

Youth violence affects everyone; no one is immune. Victims of youth violence are those who are impacted directly and indirectly. Furthermore, it is not only an inner-city problem. Suburban and rural communities across the country, which have viewed themselves as isolated from this problem, have begun to experience threats to their own peace and security. Citizens in increasing numbers are beginning to experience the effects of this problem. The problem is no longer relegated to one neighbourhood, ethnic, or socio-economic group, but is now viewed as a national public health crisis.[2] We all share in the costs exacted by youth violence. There are thousands of lives lost annually. Many children are robbed of the joys of neighborhood games and playgrounds because it is simply unsafe to play outside. Family disruptions accompany each incident of crime/violence. Financial costs average $14 000 per treatment for gunshot wounds. This amounts to $15 billion US dollars per year for handgun violence alone.[3]

Many points of view

The heightened anxiety and attention of this pandemic has lead to an abundance of studies, analyses, discussions of the issues, explanations, and recommendations. There appears to be no consensus, even among the experts, as to what is precisely the most effective approach to bringing solution to this national problem. The complexity of the problem, its magnitude, its increasing rate of growth, and its frightening impact on the citizenry and major institutions have caused some to adopt the opinion that the best approach to solving this crisis is simply to "get tough, lock up those who commit violent crimes, and throw away the key". Many of those who start out, with singleness of purpose, to conduct studies and analyses of this problem, end up with conclusions that are quite varied, even sometimes opposite.

Even with this wide variance in recommendations for curbing or preventing youth violence, there appears to be broad agreement that certain factors appear to contribute to youth violence and criminal activity. The most widely agreed upon factors include:
* lack of moral values
* poverty and chronic unemployment
* family disruptions
* racism, bigotry
* unjust restriction of opportunity
* denial of societal justice
* drug abuse and/or alcoholism
* pervasive television violence
* absence of respected authority
* low self-esteem
* absence of responsibility
* youth gang activity.

While neither of these factors, taken alone, will necessarily cause youth to be violent, there appears to be a direct correlation between high incidence of these factors and increased youth violence.

Social Institutions

The major social institutions serve us by helping us, as a society, to develop patterned and predictable ways of thinking and behaving with respect to the important aspects of lives. They help shape our beliefs, values, and norms. We have looked to them to provide leadership in confronting this challenge to our peace and stability. The family is the most natural and basic of these institutions and has the potential to impact the society more directly than any of the others.[4] Without the support of functional and involved families, all community efforts to bring solution to this problem fall short of their goals. Healthy families perform a wide range of functions for each of their members. Individual members look to a family to provide:
* physical needs (food, clothes, shelter)
* love and nurturing

* security and protection
* identity (gender, ethnic, national, etc.)
* spiritual foundation
* recognition
* a sense of belonging
* power, empowerment
* direction
* values and moral foundation
* culture
* discipline
* example
* attention, acceptance, emotional support
* socialisation and development of life skills.

This listing does not begin to cover the wide range of roles families play in meeting the needs of their members. It only lists some of the most basic roles families perform. When families, for whatever reasons, are unable to fulfil the expected roles and meet these needs, many of today's youth seek other institutions, both formal and informal, to serve as a substitute provider for the fulfilment of their needs. To be part of the solution to the problem of youth violence, families must view themselves as the first line of provision for these needs and commit, by word and deed, to be the primary influence in the lives of youth. This must happen at the individual family level, so that each family and each member has clear expectations of this critical relationship. It is essential for children and youth to know that there is a beneficial tomorrow for them.

Healthy families do not happen by coincidence; they are built for purpose. Whatever their structure, they require hard work and perseverance to be successful. In order for solid families to be built, there should exist some reason and expectation of the outcome of this building process. We can refer to this as a "vision". The importance of having clarity of focus and expectation is stated in a biblical reference: "For without a vision, the people cast off restraints."[5] Without a realistic view of what successful family building will produce, parents and other family members are reluctant to subject themselves to the restraint or discipline required to build solid and effective families. Clarity of long-termed vision provides direction and helps fuel the desire to set up and achieve short and long term goals and activities.

Obstacles to be overcome

There are many forces at work in society today which can stand as obstacles to the building of healthy and fully functioning families. Materialism can undermine the value system of families and result in an over-emphasis on money and physical possessions at the expense of the development of moral standards and meaningful human relationships. Heavy exposure to media violence contributes to aggressive behaviour in youth and fosters societal attitudes that condone violence. Families can be vulnerable to excessive reliance on the ideas and attitudes of the commercial media. The result is that families cease to think critically for themselves and are directed in the formulation of their values, world view, and personal choices by irresponsible commercial interests. Individualism and self-centredness may also be a detriment to family. The rise in divorce rates display a lack of interdependence that is the fibre of any family unit.

When families are not able to overcome these and many other obstacles, they are at risk of becoming broken and dysfunctional. They cease to provide fulfilment of the essential needs for their members. One consequence is that society is negatively impacted by youth with significant unmet needs. A common thread through the rationale given by the perpetrators of youth violence is that they are inwardly angry. This anger is fueled by a feeling of deprivation. They feel cheated of the fulfilment of essential needs, which the family should have provided. Other consequences of unhealthy families on society are increased public welfare costs, societal frustration and anger, and an increase of emotionally crippled people in the overall population. Broken families produce increased numbers of broken people.

What families can do

The focus of attention as one combats the problem of youth violence must first be on the family. The critical role which families play as the primary social institution in society cannot be overstated. Solutions to concerns such as youth violence must begin with the building of strong and fully functioning families.

It is obvious that all institutions in society have some part to play in bringing solution to this problem. None, however, are as critical as the family; for it is the family which functions as the incubator of all values and attitudes which teach peacemaking and promotes a peaceable environment in which development can take place. The everyday interactions of family living serve as an ideal laboratory in which peacemaking skills can be developed and practised. Families that have and enjoy peace can choose to export peacemaking to the larger community. The following quote supports this idea: "How a family demonstrates affection, shares power and responsibility, resolves conflicts, responds to hostility, copes with illness and injury, expresses grief, encourages achievement, conducts its common meals, spends time and money, plans its vacation and travel, forms its political opinions, confronts fears for the future, and worships or fails to worship God ... these questions make the family the potential greenhouse of all peacemaking."[6]

There are a number of practical steps which parents and other family members might take in the interest of fostering attitudes in youth which influence them to be peacemakers.

Consciously discuss issues of justice in the house

Some would say that parents' job is to protect their children, to shield them from evil until they get older, and to nurture their sense of beauty and goodness, love, and play. There is much truth to this. Yet at the same time they are being exposed to war, injustice and evil. It is on the news. It is in the movies. Toys which promote violent behavior are quite popular. Parents need to help children and youth deal with all this. Family discussions are highly recommended. Discussing issues of injustice and peace in the home can take the form of watching and discussing the news together.

Promote self-esteem and affirmation

Peacemaking requires a healthy sense of self-esteem. Self-esteem is essential for developing compassion and in caring for others. It is also essential in combating the kind of violence done to self through chemical abuse and other destructive patterns. Neither children nor adults can reach out to others if they do not feel comfortable with themselves. Further, peacemaking is sometimes a public and even a risky undertaking. No one, children or adults, is capable of going public, taking a stand for their convictions, working for change, if they do not feel good about themselves. Without self-esteem, we look for acceptance through conformity. We are afraid to stand out. Nurturing children's sense of self-esteem by affirming their efforts and by providing opportunities to develop their talents is an enormously important part of enabling them to become persons who are willing to take a stand – peacemakers.

Help children solve conflicts through non-violent methods

Children learn and use non-violent conflict resolution skills only when these skills are taught in an environment that encourages their use. Thus, families promote peacemaking skills when they make their home a place where affirmation rather than constant criticism is the norm. Specific non-violent conflict resolution or problem-solving skills can be taught from the earliest years, especially if parents allow their children to participate in family decision-making. Conflict resolution skills include listening skills, expressing rather than repressing one's feelings, and especially learning non-hurtful ways to express anger, expressing needs and wants in clear terms, weighing a number of possible solutions to any given conflict, negotiating skills. The more that parents can encourage children to use these skills and solve their own problems rather than always intervening in child-child conflicts with a quick solution, the more opportunities children have to learn these skills.

Practise cooperation

The more that family members are working together, the more peace there will be in that home. Sharing tasks rather than "everyone on their own" helps – whether it is occasional meal preparation, doing dishes, baking holiday goodies, gardening, etc. Encouraging children to share their skills with one another is another step. Examples include: helping a younger sibling learn to read, roller skate, ride a bike, do long division, or perform other skills.[7]

Conclusions

Youth violence affects negatively the quality of life for all citizens. There exists a direct link between unmet needs in youth and increases in violent criminal behaviour by youth. Fully functioning families are the ideal place where such needs are met. These families generally do not contribute to the problems of youth violence; for they offer solutions. By supporting and encouraging the building of strong families, a nation, city, or community takes a direct and effective measure to reduce and bring an end to this costly problem. Families can take steps to strengthen themselves and bring benefit to the overall society by teaching and practising peacemaking skills in the home, the community, and the nation.

References

1. Children's Defense Fund Reports. 1994. *Special Report: Violence.* Washington, D.C.
2. Trafford, Abigail. 1992. *Violence as a Public Health Crisis.* Public Welfare.
3. Confluence St. Louis. 1993. *For Our Children, For Our Future: Developing Connections to Prevent Youth Crime In the St. Louis Metropolitan Area.* St. Louis.
4. Lamanna, Mary Ann and Agnew, Riedman. *Marriage and Families.* Belmont: Wadsworth Publishing.
5. Proverbs. *New American Standard Bible.*
6. United Methodist Council of Bishops. *In Defense of Creation.*
7. McGinnis, Jim and McGinnis, Kathy. *Families Acting for Peace.* St. Louis Institute for Peace and Justice.

The role of the church in Namibia in fostering constructive attitudes in a transition to democracy

Rev. Nathan-Eliab Kapofi

Manager: Religious Programmes, Namibian Broadcasting Corporation

Abstract

The church as the body of the elect of God has been charged with the duty to make this world a better place for the people of God to live in. History has shown that the church is indeed a great agent of change. She has, through the ages, been engaged in proclaiming the Gospel, teaching, instructing, admonishing, counselling and offering material assistance to the needy. This has been, in no small measure, the practice of the church in Namibia during the time of colonial domination in mobilising the people towards transition to democratic rule. This paper will also focus on the challenges facing the church in maintaining the right attitudes and morals.

Introduction

The church's role in Namibia increased as the political situation became more and more complex and socio-economic problems mounted. The church became more vocal against evil practices of injustice perpetuated by the apartheid system. In her prophetic stand and proclamation, Luke 4:18-19 became the vivid inspirational weapon: "The Spirit of the Lord is upon me, because He has anointed me to preach good news to the poor, He has sent me to proclaim release to the captives and recovering of sight to the blind, to set at liberty those who are oppressed, to proclaim the acceptable Year of the Lord". In order for the people to realise this truth, the church intensified her programmes of teaching, preaching and social upliftment of the poor.

During the colonial era

Education

In order to help people cope with the situation at hand, education became the most important element in equipping the church. Adult literacy programmes took off with centres established countrywide. Volunteer teachers received instruction and learners ultimately took it upon themselves to fund the projects thus securing their supported continuity. Church buildings offered shelter, as projects were church related. Sunday School, Youth League, Women's and Men's Leagues had each to cater for a literacy and/or language class where illiteracy and ignorance were fought as enemies. The aim was to eliminate illiteracy and inability to understand languages like English and Afrikaans. Newspaper reading and listening to radio became practical parts of the programme.

The church also maintained her high schools which were established right at the beginning of missionary work in the country. These schools have, through the years, produced academics and professionals permeating all strata of the Namibian society as teachers, university professors, pastors, medical doctors, nurses, engineers, lawyers, magistrates, business people, government ministers, secretaries, army and police officers, pilots, ambassadors, yes, even the State President. These are the living testimonies to our slogan "Education is the key".

Preaching

With the situational change the preaching method of the church did not remain static. Preachers adopted a tough attitude to a rough situation, became more bold in their evangelisation, pragmatic, prophetic and aggressive in approach. The biblical interpretation became vigorous and revivals were held everywhere. Church buildings were packed to capacity every Sunday morning with people who came to lay down their heavy burdens at the foot of the cross of the Lord of life. There was no place where the church's presence was not felt. A bed-ridden patient, out-patient, hospital worker or visitor would always hear the preaching of the Word by a pastor, hospital chaplain or a member of the hospital staff.

It was in Bible study groups that the Word was studied in depth and answers sought to questions daily haunting the hearts, minds and feelings of the people of God.

Counselling

Many counselling opportunities are sought by parishioners. These are important teaching moments. Education of engaged couples for marriages, family counselling, counselling of troubled marriage partners, parent counselling and even bereavement counselling have included teaching aspects on human dignity, self-respect, self-worth, mutual respect, faithfulness, responsibility and love for one another.

Ecumenism

The need to face the common enemy enhanced the idea of the church to put together forces. It became imperative for the church not only to speak on behalf of the otherwise voiceless, powerless, oppressed people but with one united unwavering voice, to witness to the truth of the liberating gospel. To that end ties at the ecumenical front became very strong.

Interdenominational meetings, gatherings and conferences were held where strategies were devised on how to resist the oppressive regime and how to prepare the masses effectively for the transition to democratic rule. Political meetings and rallies were addressed by clergy on important topics like suffering, endurance, courage, hope, liberation, salvation, love for neighbour and enemy, forgiveness, acceptance and reconciliation. When the now governing party declared forgiveness and reconciliation as their policy it did not fall on foreign soil. Although it was difficult for the people to live up to the policy in practice, they gradually got used to living with it.

Whatever harsh conditions, whatever inhuman and unjust treatment they had suffered and endured became part of their unforgotten heroic history. One human aspect that ever remains is that, unlike God, people can forgive but do not forget.

One major front at which the church in Namibia visibly demonstrated their ecumenism and unity is the Council of Churches in Namibia (CCN) to which they affiliated. The CCN became a strong voice of the people advocating their cause. It is through the CCN that the church embarked upon social programmes, such as adult continuing education, housing, health education and services and literacy, technical training, water supply and legal advice through regionally established human rights centres. The CCN also offered training to people, encouraged and assisted them to run community projects such as agricultural gardens, bricklaying and sewing. Many of the self-help projects helped people discover their potential, appreciate their selfhood and worth, instilled and developed their self- and mutual respect, their dignity and somebodiness.

Training

Theological, pastoral and lay preacher training focused on equipping the people to present the Word of God to the people in such a contextual manner that it provided the answers relevant to their questions. Whereas churches each had their own training institutions in the sixties, the United Evangelical Lutheran Theological Seminary, Paulinum, became a joint venture towards church unity. In order to widen and enrich the diversity of the church some candidates attended Lutheran, Anglican, Catholic and other interdenominational seminaries here in southern Africa and abroad in Britain and the United States of America.

The church's 1971 open letter to the then South African Prime Minister, the late Honourable B.J. Vorster, became the pivot of all the revolutionary and patriotic thinking and acting of the masses in Namibia. This letter, signed by the late Bishop Dr Leonard Auala of the Evangelical Lutheran Owambo-Kavango Church, now the Evangelical Lutheran Church in Namibia (ELCIN), and the late Rev. Paulus Gowaseb, moderator of the Evangelical Lutheran Church (Rhenish Mission), now the Evangelical Lutheran Church in the Republic of Namibia (ELCRN), shed more light on the plight of the Namibian people to the international community. On their part the Namibian people took it upon themselves to strive for the respect of their human dignity, basic human rights, better living wages, better working and living conditions and, most of all, respect for human life.

While the agonised people were shouting "What have we done?", the church raised the voice to the oppressor "Let my people go that they may serve me" (Exodus 8:1; 9:1; 10: 3).

During the independence process and post-independence

The church had walked hand in hand with the people through the difficult situation during the colonial period, offering support, teaching, instruction, admonishing, counselling and offering material assistance to the needy and mobilising the people toward transition to democracy. People came to understand the real meaning of the proverbial expression, "A friend in need is a friend indeed": They put their total trust in God who was "able to deliver them from the burning fiery furnace" (Daniel 3:17), to whom the church was a strong living witness.

With the implementation of the UN Resolution 435 of 1978 which secured the return of the Namibian exiles and the ultimate free and fair elections resulting in the independence of the Republic, no one could be entrusted the major responsibility of receiving the returnees, but the church.

The work of repatriation, reception and rehabilitation under the auspices of the CCN was kept on hold after the congregations took over the task of welcoming returnees in their midst and introduced them to their families and relatives. It was at these festivals that the ruling party's policy of forgiveness and reconciliation was more emphasised in order to break the hostility, negativity and fear held by various relatives belonging to different political camps. Such attitudes urged the church to reinforce her home-based Bible instruction involving family members. These programmes later extended to involving numerous neighbouring families and ultimately the whole village. It was on these occasions that people were instructed to tolerate, love and help one another as compatriots.

Voters' education was imparted to them as well as how to live in peace in order to rebuild, reconstruct and develop the country.

The constitution of the Republic of Namibia became the textbook in various parochial schools, like Sunday School, confirmation classes, adult Bible classes, Youth League, Women's League, Men's League as well as in premarital and family counselling sessions. Everybody was made to understand their democratic rights, not only politically, but also from the biblical point of view, with the understanding that democracy, like charity, starts at home, in the family.

Challenges

The church in Namibia is facing great challenges in maintaining the right attitudes and morals. In any society there are always some social phenomena which cannot be eliminated totally .

In Namibia unemployment has frustrated many young people. A good number of them are employing the skills imparted to them by the church in self-help projects like brick-laying, building construction, agriculture, electrical repair, mechanical work, photography, art, etc. Some others, unfortunately, feel it is their democratic right to choose not to work but to claim a share of other people's property. The consequences of such attitudes are house-breaking, armed robbery, wanton killings and car theft.

The influx from rural areas to urban centres, especially to the capital city, has caused acute housing shortages. Overcrowded living conditions have manifested health hazards such as meningitis and cholera. Malnutrition has taken its toll among the small children since mothers cannot provide good food. Alcohol abuse has resulted in sexual misbehaviour with a high rate of teenage pregnancy and extramarital relationships, abortion, marriage breakdowns and the AIDS endemic.

These and many other social concerns are not left unattended to. In his speeches the President of the Republic of Namibia, Dr Sam Nujoma, is constantly urging the nation to work hard in order to fight the three basic enemies facing them, namely, ignorance, hunger and diseases.

Various church activities have indicated the reactivated efforts to boost the moral attitudes of the people. The Prime Minister of Namibia, the Right Honourable Hage Geingob, convened an inter-religions consultation on how to deal with the situation in the country. This was followed by an interdenominational church conference on "Morality: not an option but a must" organised by the Dutch Reformed Church in Namibia. The CNN convenes, at regular intervals, consultations between various church groups, the NGOs, Government Ministries and the Ministry of Home Affairs specifically, with the Police, to devise means and methods of combating crime.

It is important for me to mention the great achievement of our radio and television programmes in helping to foster attitudes. Our religious programmes consist of worshipping, educational, informative, entertainment and counselling categories, targeting all social groups in all nine language groups. What matters is not that we are in a position to reach almost everybody. The most important thing of all is the content of the message that is broadcast: the message of repentance. Preachers must stop preaching people out of hell, and preach hell out of the people.

People should change their attitudes. They have to repent and they must hear that message from the church constantly. No multitudes and troops of well-trained soldiers with sophisticated modern weaponry can change the attitudes of the people, but the sharp Word of God can cause their hearts to change. That is the thing most desired by the Lord God who says "If my people who are called by my name humble themselves, and pray and seek my face, and turn from their wicked ways, then I will hear from heaven, and will forgive their sin and heal their land" (2 Chron. 7:14).

Towards true reconciliation

Dr L Alberts
Co-chairman: Rustenburg Conference

Abstract

A basic requirement for the future welfare and success of the New South Africa is true reconciliation between the various groupings in our population. The first requisite for reconciliation is a basic change of attitude. Those wrong attitudes that have developed and been built up over centuries and in some cases escalated over the past few decades must be altered radically. Without such a change of heart we may experience suspended hostilities and temporary peace but no lasting solutions.

The South African case is by no means hopeless. An analysis of the situation in the time of Christ indicates that the inhabitants of Palestine were even more polarised than we ever were in this country. Things were pretty tough when we consider the mutual attitudes of Jews, Greeks, Romans, Samaritans and Canaanites. However, in this very situation Christ appeared on the scene and Paul used this historical setting to illustrate how the gospel message can bring about a change of attitude amongst various ethnic groupings. Moreover, the potential change was demonstrated to be applicable in real situations. The gospel was not merely a theoretical pie in the sky when it came to human relations but effective in a down-to-earth manner.

As scientific discoveries have to be demonstrated on pilot plant scale before they can find commercial application, so the church will have to become God's pilot plant to demonstrate how effective the gospel can be in furthering reconciliation in South Africa.

South Africa is a multi-ethnic society. Over three centuries and especially in the second half of this century polarisation and antagonisms developed between some of these ethnic groupings. This has led to mistrust and even hate and violence, of which we are all poignantly aware.

It is readily concluded that if the New South Africa is to achieve successful development, harmony and peace, true reconciliation between the various groupings is an obvious, unavoidable requirement. Before successful reconciliation between any two parties can be achieved, a basic change of attitude is a prerequisite. Those wrong attitudes that have developed in the past and even escalated in the latter decades in our country must be altered radically. Without such a change of heart we may manage to suspend hostilities temporarily, but no lasting peace can be expected.

We are inclined to think that our situation is uniquely complex and difficult. This is not so. Let us analyse the situation in the country where Christ was born some 2 000 years ago. There were the Jews, a conquered but very proud people. After all, they were the chosen race of God and therefore above all other nations. Because they had the knowledge and tradition of worshipping God all other peoples were referred to as heathens. The cultured Greeks who were the world leaders in the sciences and the arts, as well as the Romans who were the political and military leaders of the world, detested the Jews for their haughty attitude. The Israelis in turn hated the Romans as conquerors and suppressors in their own country. Add to this situation the presence of Samaritans, the religious half-castes of the day. They held onto the first five books of the Old Testament but beyond that added non-Judaistic beliefs. The Jews really despised the Samaritans. Another grouping was the natives of the country, i.e., the Canaanites. They were the low class labourers at times referred to as dogs. In addition the country experienced its share of rebels, terrorists and bandits. Barabbas and the two crucified together with Christ were prime examples.

With this background setting Paul and his fellow apostles started sharing the Gospel of Christ on worldwide scale in the face of tremendous obstacles. Paul boldly proclaimed the unity of Jews, Greeks, males, females, slaves and free men in Christ Jesus. He preached that the wall of separation between Jews and Gentiles had been broken down by Christ.

It is worth spending a few moments on this concept. The Jewish temple with its various courtyards and chambers was accessible to Jews but not to non-Jews. At a given point a barrier in the form of a wall kept out all heathens. If one of the latter was found on the inside of this wall he could be killed. So severe was the polarisation. God was not available to non-Jews. Paul states in Ephesians 2:14 that Christ, through his death, broke down the walls of division between Jew and non-Jew.

A fascinating piece of history is described in the 10th chapter of the book of Acts. It is the story of Peter the Jewish apostle and Cornelius, a Roman. The latter was an earnest seeker of the way of salvation. On a given day, the account tells us, an angel appeared and instructed Cornelius to send for Peter who was staying at the time in the house of Simon the tanner in the town of Joppe some distance away. Cornelius obeyed immediately.

In the meantime Peter, whilst staying with Simon, had a vision of a huge sheet descending from heaven and on the sheet a number of ceremonially unclean animals. A voice from heaven instructed Peter to kill and eat. Peter refused because this was very much against Jewish law. After the voice spoke a third time, telling Peter that what God calls clean he dare not regard as unclean, the Jewish apostle was very perplexed. What was God trying to tell him? At that moment the messengers from Cornelius arrived with the invitation to Peter to come and share his knowledge of Christ with their boss. Suddenly Peter realised what the vision meant. Normally he would never enter a Roman home because in terms of Jewish law it was unclean. Now God told him to go regardless. The rest of the story indicates Peter's total change of attitude and a tremendously successful interaction with Cornelius that ended in true fellowship.

The evidence can be multiplied over and over again. A real personal relationship with Christ can lead towards a right attitude that is the prerequisite for lasting reconciliation and peace between persons at cross purposes who may differ culturally in terms of norms and traditions.

Where does all this reasoning take us? Can the message of the Christian gospel ever find application in the 20th century world? It may be beautiful and true but how can one get it to work out in our society?

Let us consider an illustration from science and industry. If a scientist makes a discovery in a laboratory such as a new method of extracting aluminium from the ore, one would never persuade a company to apply this new method on large scale. No one in his right mind will invest say R1 billion in a commercial plant based merely on a scientist's discovery in a research laboratory. What is required to convince such a company is a successful pilot plant demonstration of the practical feasibility of the new discovery. Test tubes and electronic devices used in the laboratory must now be replaced by pumps, pipes, drums and electric motors. In fact a miniature plant must be designed in which the process is tested. In such a procedure adjustments will be made, scale up parameters evaluated etc. Once this has been successfully accomplished the pilot plant results can be presented to the company in question who can then confidently consider a large scale commercial operation.

The application of the parable is simple. God's great perfect experiment providing the basis for reconciliation between man and God as well as between man and man was performed some two thousand years ago on the Cross of Calvary. The question arises: How can this be demonstrated on pilot plant scale? And the answer is: the Christian church. It is unreasonable to expect the real world out there to turn to the Christian message for answers if it does not see it operate successfully on pilot plant scale in the church. This places an awesome responsibility but also tremendous opportunity in the hands of the church.

Who or what is this entity called the church? Is it a building, a group of bishops or pastors in some gathering such as a synod or an assembly? Not really. The true church is made up of Christ's followers. As a corporate body they can be the instruments of reconciliation and peace.

The school's contribution to peace and development

Dr E Hugh Davies
Head: Education Coordination Service

Abstract

The school has a role to play both as a cradle of peace and also as a cradle of development. Its role in contributing to development is perhaps rather clearer than its role as an agent for transforming individuals into peace-loving, peace-seeking and peace-practising South Africans, but the view expressed in this paper is that the school can make a contribution in both areas. In order to make that contribution, however, some major shifts of emphasis, orientation and approach will be necessary.

If the school is to promote the development of peace, for example, certain essential qualities in teachers, in the organisational structure of schools and in the formal curriculum will have to be given a good deal of attention. There must also be a recognition that it may not be possible for the school to address value and attitudinal change, especially in older learners.

If the school is to play as definitive a role in development as it probably can, there will need to be a reappraisal of which areas of personal development need urgent attention and could be dealt with by the education sector, as well as of the entire curriculum and its pivotal role in developing generic skills of a kind related to the world of work.

For those shifts to happen, there will have to be a very clear vision within society as to what the role of the school should be in these areas; there will have to be a commitment to trying to achieve those goals on the part both of the teaching profession and also that of other role-players; and social agencies like the church and the family will have to do their part to assist the education system to achieve a transformation which it cannot hope to accomplish on its own.

Introduction

The title of this paper – "The school's contribution to peace and development" – makes a number of assumptions. The most obvious of these are that the school *can* make a contribution to the advancement of the cause of peace and that it *can* contribute to development. A less overt assumption is that development may not be possible unless there is peace and order.

The title of the paper also has to be placed within the context of the overall theme of the conference, which deals with the role of the family, the church and school in fostering attitudes that will lead to peace and development. There is an explicit recognition, therefore, that the work which is

49

done in schools cannot be seen in isolation from the wider social context in general, and from the specific contexts of family and moral and value development in particular.

Although this paper concentrates on the role of the school as one of the cradles of peace and development, the observations made should always be seen in the context of that wider matrix of social institutions and interactions which constitutes the world of the learner.

Two aspects will be dealt with here: the school as one of the cradles of peace; and the school as one of the cradles of development.

The school's contribution to peace

A key question which has to be addressed is whether schools can make a contribution to peace and harmony at all. Most of the members of this audience will be familiar with the vast array of literature on what has been called "the blackboard jungle". No-one who has an interest in education will be unaware of the organisational and institutional difficulties which exist in large numbers of schools, in developing and developed countries alike – schools in which gangs are alive and well, schools in which violence is commonplace, schools in which teachers and pupils alike often require the protection of security personnel. These places exist. Comparative educationists in certain quarters have long accepted Sadler's dictum that "the things that happen outside the schools matter much more than the things which happen inside the schools". If these statements were valid in an unqualified sense, we should have to admit that schools cannot make a difference.

And yet there is compelling evidence that schools can, and do, make a difference. How does it come about that in Bosnia there are schools which are not torn asunder and to which children love to go as places where they can escape much of what is happening in society around them? How is it that within schools there are havens to which the pupils love to go?

To the question as to whether schools can make a difference, specifically with regard to developing a climate of peace and attitudes of co-operation rather than of conflict, there is therefore no simple answer. Evidence available indicates that there are some schools that make a difference and others which do not.

What preconditions therefore have to be satisfied for the school to make a difference at all?

I would like to suggest that there are three main preconditions, as well as some subsidiary ones which will not be referred to here.

1. The first of these is a caring, dedicated corps of teaching and other personnel – men and women of calibre who care for the traumatised pupils who come into the school; who are concerned for the general improvement of the lot of their pupils; and who are willing to subordinate their own personal concerns to the needs of their pupils. It is an interesting fact that many people, when they recall their schooldays insofar as they recall them at all, tend to remember individual teachers who for whatever reason made a particular impression, whether for good or for ill. My first postulate is that the school can make a difference in developing a climate of peace only if the care, concern and empathy which are necessary human qualities in a peace-loving, peace-pursuing and peace-practising environment are present. And those qualities have to be characteristic of the educators in the system in the first instance. But this is not enough.

2. In the second place, if it is tenable that the development of an environment conducive to peace is dependent on human qualities, values and attitudes, then it needs to be remembered that, in the main, values are caught rather than taught. Quite apart, therefore, from individual qualities which personnel need to bring to their task, there is the further imperative that the organisational climate of the school, its ethos and its unspoken rules, should testify to fairness, justice, and non-adversarial approaches to problem-resolution. Children do what they see their elders doing. Children learn their attitudes to life at least in part from their elders. And they develop their understandings of organisational culture at least in part on the basis of the organisational culture they are exposed to day by day. That organisational culture is the school. The non-formal curriculum of the school is therefore a crucial factor in the process of attitudinal development and change. That non-formal curriculum does not simply happen – it is brought about by the way in which the principal interacts with the personnel and they with the principal; by the way in which a value and attitudinal climate is developed; by the way in which the interactions of pupils with each other and with the personnel are mediated and dealt with.

3. A third prerequisite is a moral imperative. This, I know, will not be a fashionable statement. There are those who would deny that there are certain universal human values, who would want to argue that the school is the last place which should be dealing with issues of values and so on. I am not one of them. I firmly believe that unless our value systems are such that positive orientations to peace and reconciliation form a part of them, we shall forever be an unhappy people, forever at odds with one another because we are at odds with our own inner beings. If our society wants to be at peace

with itself and with the world, if we want our children to be at peace with themselves and with one another, it is my conviction that we shall have to ensure that the formal curriculum in schools makes provision for the teaching of those values and attitudes which we know to be conducive to advancing the cause of peace.

I therefore believe that the formal curriculum needs to be re-examined. We need to eliminate from it much that might contribute to attitudes not conducive to positive relationships between the peoples of South Africa; we need to add to it much that will contribute to the forging of a single nation with a single set of purposes, one of these being to live at peace with everybody.

What I have said thus far may sound far too simple and even naïve. We can afford to be neither. We come from a deeply divided society. The divisions, the scars, the animosities all run deep. There are deeply emotional questions which have to be dealt with. These include questions such as why *should* I forgive; why *should* I forget; I *will* avenge myself and so on. I would not pretend that there are easy answers to these questions, but they have to be found by each man, woman and child in this country, and the skills to put those answers into practice have to be acquired by all of us.

We need, however, to recognise that the capacity of schools to influence young people appears to diminish in inverse proportion to the age of those pupils – the older the pupil, the less the chance of materially shaping attitudes and values. We need also to recognise that many of the young people in our schools are adults – they have left adolescence behind and are themselves in some cases parents. In other societies they would not still be at school. We need in my opinion to do a good deal of work on what the best way is of coping with the educational needs of these young people, and to analyse the extent to which the conventional school is an appropriate means for addressing those needs.

Despite this reservation, it is nevertheless my view that schools can make a difference provided the three preconditions I have mentioned are satisfied: that there be a corps of educators who are deeply committed to their pupils and to making a contribution to the healing of our society; that there be an organisational climate in our schools and classrooms which turns them into havens of peace for those who move within their walls; and that conscious steps be taken to amend the curriculum in such a way that the development of knowledge, skills and attitudes conducive to the development of a peace-loving, peace-seeking and peace-practising nation is actively promoted and fostered.

The school's contribution to development

The second main issue addressed by this paper deals with the school's contribution to development. There are at least two issues here. The first of these concerns the development of the individual as a person. The second concerns that aspect called by some "human resource development" – that is, equipping the individual to play a role in society, including successful entry to the economy through the world of work.

Development of the individual

Perhaps one of the major criticisms of our school curriculum – and I believe that in one sense it is a justified criticism – is that the curriculum is largely irrelevant to the needs of the majority of pupils. That criticism seems to stem especially from employers, whose interest is more focussed on the ability of an entrant to the labour force to do a job of work as quickly as possible. But the question which also needs to be asked is whether the curriculum addresses the needs of the individual, and helps to develop that person.

Major issues in our society at present include the surging AIDS problem, drug abuse, violence, deprivation, lawlessness, a lack of respect for human life and property, the rejection of authority and a number of other serious difficulties. The question to be asked is whether the curriculum attempts to equip pupils to deal with these issues, not merely as abstract issues but as issues which impact on their daily lives.

There are probably as many views on this matter as there are commentators on it. My own view, which is admittedly contestable, is that by and large we do not adequately prepare pupils to deal with these issues in any kind of consistent and personal way. Furthermore, I am not sure that we prepare them to deal with other more mundane but necessary issues: how to manage their money; how to plan their time; how to open a bank account; how to develop safe habits on the road, including driver training; how to manage sexuality in close interpersonal relationships and so on. There are many who argue that most of these issues are the responsibility of the home, or the responsibility of the church, or the responsibility of some other agency, or the shared responsibility of any agencies other than the school. If that is so, then I think we have to say that those agencies have not done a particularly good job. The fabric of our society has been strained, and in the process not necessarily positively affected, for a very long time now. What, if anything, should the education system be doing about it?

Much of what pupils learn at school, especially in secondary schools, seems to be product-oriented – that is, related to learning facts, writing tests on those facts, and passing examinations. The aim of schooling, for many, appears to be to pass examinations. Surely there has to be more to it than that? The question is not so much what you know, as what you *do* with what you know – that is, how it is applied. Much of what pupils are exposed to does not require them to develop higher-order cognitive skills such as those of analysis, synthesis and application.

In a nutshell, what I am saying is that we are not necessarily doing as well as we might in assisting young people to develop as human beings.

What of the other area of development I mentioned?

Development of the capacity necessary to enter the workforce

More than one survey has shown that employers are quite happy to employ a person who is trainable, even though he or she lacks the specific skills required to do a particular job. But what is critical is that the person in question be trainable. Survey after survey indicates that all too many of our school leavers are not trainable other than at great expense, because they lack the generic skills that employers expect. Essential skills relevant to appropriate vocational and on-the-job training are simply not well developed, and may even be entirely absent. International reports on our country's level of competitiveness, on our success in developing human resources and related issues, indicate that we are not doing anywhere nearly as well as we ought to be.

Another sad reality in our fractured society is that we have so many young people who have not had access to schooling, and that there are so many adults who have been denied the empowering experience of literacy and numeracy in the kind of society where these are crucial first-stage skills in the process of self-improvement.

We therefore need to enhance access while at the same time doing a more effective task to ensure that we optimise the opportunities for teaching and learning to which learners in this country can be exposed.

Against this background, it is clear that we need a massive process of curriculum review together with a shift of emphasis. This will require the redirection of the skills of teachers, as well as considerable effort to reorientate both pupils and parents to the reality that many facets of the school curriculum in South Africa at present prepare learners only for one thing – that is, further study.

Quite apart from curriculum issues, however, there is also the very important area of methodological issues. The way in which teachers tackle material to be dealt with can have a significant effect on the way in which learners internalise material and on the extent to which they apply it. If the learner engages with the teacher in meaningful discourse, the nature of that interaction has a profound impact on what is learned and on how it is learned. If the learner is merely confronted with a section in a textbook and told to learn it, the interaction between the learner and the material as well as the understanding of its significance is of a quite different character.

The methodological paradigm which has tended to be followed in many South African schools has not been conducive to the kind of discourse which is empowering to the individual and which encourages the development of interactive skills. Quite apart, therefore, from the necessity to revise the curriculum, we shall have to mount programmes which will enable teachers to review their own teaching skills and to move into a mode more appropriate to the concept of human development.

Then, too, the teaching support materials that are available may also require reappraisal. A businessman remarked to me recently that he always found it frustrating that in textbooks which were teaching young children about money, the word sums often said things like "You go to the shop with R5. You take a litre of milk costing R2 and a loaf of bread costing R1,90. How much change will the shopkeeper give you?" He pointed out that this kind of sum always makes the child the customer, and never the businessman. Why not, he asked, orientate children to entrepreneurial skills by writing the same sum "A customer gives you R5 to pay for a litre of milk costing R2 and a loaf of bread costing R1,90. How much change will you have to give the customer?" Why not, indeed?

What I am saying is that education has a crucial role to play in the process of development. By empowering individuals and giving them appropriate generic skills, the education system can do much to contribute to overall development in our society. But if it is to make the contribution that it could ideally make, substantial revision of material, redirection of the curriculum and reorientation of teaching personnel will be required.

Conclusion

The school has a role to play both as a cradle of peace and as a cradle of development. Its role in contributing to development is perhaps rather clearer than its role as an agent for transforming individuals into peace-loving, peace-seeking and peace-practising South Africans, but the view expressed in this paper is that the school can make a contribution in both areas.

In order to make that contribution, however, some major shifts of emphasis, orientation and approach will be necessary. For those shifts to happen, there will have to be a very clear vision within society as to what the role of the school should be in these areas; there will have to be a commitment to trying to achieve those goals on the part of the teaching profession and also that of other role-players; and social agencies like the church and the family will have to do their part to assist the education system to achieve a transformation which it cannot hope to accomplish on its own.

Peace-keeping: an ongoing challenge for the democratic state

Prof. Marinus Wiechers
Principal and Vice-chancellor: Unisa

Abstract

Peace-keeping implies active measures, not only to maintain and protect peace, but also to promote and ensure a peaceful state of affairs. This paper, whilst stressing the underlying values and attitudes which assure peace, concentrates on the political and constitutional instruments which a government of a democratic state has at its disposal to keep the peace. First and foremost, such a government, in order to keep the peace, must protect and enforce human rights, and, in an open, accountable way, strive for the socio-economic upliftment of the people. In extreme cases, when the foundations of democracy – which are freedom, equality and justice – are threatened, a government may apply emergency measures and even declare a state of national defence. However, in all these circumstances, it remains the free, democratic state which has to be defended. Emergency powers may never, in the name of peace-keeping, be abused to safeguard privilege, domination or other undemocratic practices.

Introduction

Human behaviour and attitudes must be conducted according to certain accepted norms. Law, which primarily has to regulate human behaviour and interpersonal relationships, is a set and pre-defined body of norms which can be enforced by the state and its institutions.

In establishing that set of normative rules which we call the body of laws, the legislature proceeds from an ideal state of affairs. For instance, rules of family law will be based on an idea or notion of the accepted, well-organised family with its approved value system, and will regulate matters pertaining to family affairs in such a way that the image of that accepted, well-organised family is protected. Child abuse, neglect and other behaviour which can threaten sound family life are proscribed. If a marriage, which is still considered to be the protective environment for sound family life, irretrievably breaks down, the law also has to regulate that catastrophic event in such a way that the interests of the spouses and especially those of the children are not neglected. In other words, the law, in regulating human behaviour, takes as its point of departure an ideal state of affairs – which in the case of family law is the normal, peaceful nuclear family with both parents in the home – but at the same time, must provide for the occurrence of unhappy events which render that ideal state of affairs impossible.

In state matters the same principles apply. Constitutional law assumes an ideal, democratic state in which the organs of state are well-organised and well-functioning and in which all citizens are well-behaved. Moreover, the normative set of constitutional rules, as embodied in the constitution, takes as its point of departure a society in which peace reigns.

At the same time, however, constitutional law must take cognisance of the fact that, in all states, there are many disruptive forces which threaten the state and its institutions and which can throw societies in turmoil and despair, or worse, which can threaten the existence of the democratic state itself. This is particularly true in the democratic state: a democracy promotes freedom; what if that freedom is abused by individuals and groups to destroy the freedom of others or to jeopardise the very existence of the democratic state? Must the state then turn to undemocratic means to protect democracy? This is what I propose to deal with in this paper, namely, the very difficult and often agonising question of how the democratic state protects and ensures its democratic nature in the face of violent and disruptive forces. In short, how does a democracy protect state security?

Peace-keeping in the democratic state

A democratic state cannot be fully realised unless conditions in that state are peaceful. A state in turmoil cannot attract foreign investment and it cannot promote socio-economic development. Also, sound family and societal relations cannot be ensured if societies are beset with violence and disorder.

Often, when the whole matter of state security is raised, people tend to think of drastic, exceptional measures such as the declaration of a state of emergency, suspension of liberties and freedoms and the incarceration of unruly elements.

What is forgotten is that the democratic state's most important and effective means of protecting peace and state security, is to apply peaceful measures. Peaceful measures to protect peace and state security are those state actions which promote socio-economic upliftment, educational advancement and, generally, serve to ameliorate the quality of life. Happy and contented people are peaceful people. In this respect, the recognition and protection of individual rights and liberties are of the utmost importance, since the individual is the single most important minority in the state, and before we can even speak of the rights of collectivities, the rights of individuals composing such minorities must take prevalence.

In fulfilling its task to ensure peace and stability, the democratic state constantly tries to empower people to improve the quality of their lives. By protecting freedom of expression, assembly and association and by allowing people to contract freely, the state creates the possibilities for people to contract, negotiate and bargain and shape their own destinies. A true democracy, in essence, consists of thousands of voluntary accords between individuals and groups. For example, to ensure peace in the workplace, free association and collective bargaining are the most effective means to create conditions of stability and growth which are based on sound employer-employee relations.

At the same time, however, the state must combat those many elements in its midst which constantly threaten peace and stability. Crime, violence, public expressions of hatred, corruption and moral decline are all factors which insidiously and constantly undermine societal peace. Vigilant policing is therefore a vital ingredient of the democratic state.

A democratic state must also be aware that a serious state of affairs can develop which jeopardises the general security and peace. In such an occurrence, the government must take drastic measures and, if necessary, proclaim a state of emergency. A state of emergency, it is said, is the hour of the executive since it is not parliament or the courts which can take drastic measures, but the executive arm of government which has the force and means to act decisively. What is of the utmost importance during these times of emergency, is that the executive is effectively controlled and that executive government does not turn into government by blind force. Basic human rights must not be trampled upon and the executive must still be subjected to judicial control. In the new South African Constitution it is furthermore stipulated that a state of emergency, after three weeks, may only be extended for three months at a time, if allowed by a two-thirds majority in the National Assembly.

Finally, a state may find itself in a position that internal peace is threatened or indeed destroyed by outside forces and invasion. In such a case, international law, which outlawed war as a means of resolving state conflicts, allows for drastic measures for self-defence. Self-defence in international law must obey international conventions and is under the control of the Security Council of the United Nations.

Conclusion

No state can survive if it relies on force to maintain peace and stability. The democratic state builds on those healthy foundations of society which are the real cradles of peace. In South Africa, for many decades, state security was used as a pretext to protect and guard an iniquitous system of racial domination. The challenge of a democratic South Africa will be to foster all those institutions of peace which are the real instruments of stability and progress.

Peace and development:
challenges and role of youth

Sen. Rev. K Musa Zondi
Youth leader;
Associate Editor: Ilanga

Abstract

A good foundation for the fostering of positive attitudes to peace, is a stable family. However, all families, no matter how stable they may be, exist within a certain context which is the community or society in which they are lodged. Peace is necessary for development, and development enhances and promotes a climate conducive to peace. Youth have specific roles in the promotion of peace and development. They can, however, fully play their role only if they have been properly prepared for it by family and community. The youth potential for development has not been fully tapped. But they also face development challenges and difficulties. It is therefore important for us to examine this role and the challenges facing the youth in matters of peace and development.

I must begin by congratulating the organisers of this conference for choosing such an appropriate and relevant topic as a guiding theme. South Africa has never had a democratically elected government acceptable to most of her citizens. Now she does. The next challenge is what the theme of this conference is all about, namely; PEACE and DEVELOPMENT with particular reference to the roles that the family, the church and the school can play in cultivating and encouraging attitudes that promote these.

As a black person, I have always understood the struggle for liberation to be falling into two main phases; that is, the phase for political emancipation, and the second phase being the struggle for development.

I was brought up in a political tradition which decries Kwame Nkruma's political injunction of "seek ye first the political kingdom, and everything else will follow", as one of the most unfortunate political statements ever made on the continent of Africa. It had dire consequences for the development impetus in the then new African nations which had just freed themselves from the bondage of colonialism.

The reason why we regard this statement to have been unfortunate, is because of our deep conviction that *political freedom is meaningless without economic well-being.* In South Africa today, those of us who have been oppressed, have gained our political emancipation, but the stark reality which still confronts us, is that we are still a very long way from achieving economic well-being. That is why I said the organisers of this conference must be congratulated for choosing what is to me a very suitable theme at this point in time in South Africa.

Now that we have, in the Government of National Unity, a democratically elected government, we must face up squarely to the challenge which calls upon us to bring about development and peace in our troubled land. Now that we have a legitimate government we must tackle development challenges so that the promises of freedom could be fulfilled. The vexing question is, of course, that of peace. For development to take off, a climate of peace is necessary. This question becomes even more vexing because there is another argument which says that unless you have development, it is very difficult to promote peace. This then, in a sense, renders the subject a contentious chicken and egg argument.

However, I believe very strongly that the family, the church and the school all have a very crucial role to play in our society today in cultivating and promoting attitudes conducive to peace and development. I say so as one among many who have gone through the mill of these three institutions.

In examining the role of and the challenges facing youth in the promotion of peace and development, I want to begin by saying that a good foundation for the fostering of positive attitudes to peace and development is a stable family. However, all families, no matter how stable they may be, exist within a certain context, which is the community or society in which they are lodged. It is this context which to a certain extent determines the degree of success or failure of a family in its mission.

Part of the context that I am talking about is the church and the school. These to me form part of the context with which every family interfaces. The most important question which we must ask ourselves therefore is: What is the condition of this context? In other words, what is the situation like in our churches and schools? What is the situation like in our communities? Is it conducive to the fostering of attitudes which lead to peace and development? Are our churches and schools effective agents of peace and development?

I am mindful of the fact that though the family is the primary unit of society, the advent of single parenthood as a result of the high rate of divorce and the increasing rate of teenage pregnancies, renders it difficult to take it for granted that, with strong and stable families, all will go well. We now have very many children who do not know what it is to grow up in a stable family context.

This, taken together with the disruption of the normal fabric of society, particularly of black society, as manifested in the collapse of some of its vital structures and institutions, does not make the job of parents easy.

Many of you should know how difficult it is to rear children and youth in a society whose vital institutions have been seriously undermined. Many of you should know how difficult it is for teachers to teach kids who have lost all respect for them.

We have a serious problem of violence in this country, and it is a very difficult problem to solve. And I agree with the organisers of this conference that unless the family did their share in promoting and fostering attitudes that lead to peace, there can be no magical formula to minimise levels of violence in this country. That is where people should primarily be orientated properly. This leaves us with a challenge to look into the situation and condition of these institutions.

However, our youth are not to be found in the family, the church and the school only, they are also to be found among their peers, in youth clubs, formal and informal, in youth organisations of various kinds, and especially in political organisations, particularly when it comes to black youth. These too, together with the church and the school, should play some role in fostering attitudes that will lead to peace and development.

Some of the children and youth are not to be found in any of these institutions and situations. They are to be found in the streets of our cities and towns. These too have to be reached, and reintegrated back into the normal institutions of society where positive attitudes to peace and development could be fostered.

I believe very strongly that youth have a role to play in the promotion of peace and development. Youth are a very influential segment of society, especially in the black community. However, they will not just play that role without being properly prepared for it by the various institutions in the community.

Specific programmes need to be designed to prepare youth for peace and development. And once prepared, we need to think about how youth could be deployed into campaigns aimed at promoting peace and development.

Maybe we need to think about a *Youth Peace and Development Corps* as a vehicle to deploy our youth constructively in efforts to promote peace. Maybe we need to think about how we could strengthen family ties so as to maintain a healthy growing environment for the youth and children. Perhaps we need to look afresh at what our churches could do and are doing and see what improvements can be made. We certainly cannot stand by idly and not sort out problems that there are in our schools, particularly black schools, so that these could be turned around to get employed effectively in the promotion of peace and development.

I believe very strongly that the development potential of our youth has not been fully tapped. There is more good that the youth could do than is often realised, given opportunities to do so.

But youth face numerous challenges and difficulties too. Unemployment, lack of schooling opportunities, drugs and other forms of social deviance. These have to be tackled if our youth are to grow up into responsible citizens.

Some problems that encompass the youth are to be found in the family. Some youth grow up in homes with a lot of violence. Others grow up in homes where parents use drugs and liquor excessively. Some youth grow up exposed to a culture of low and loose morals. All these things do contribute to the various deviant characters that manifest themselves as problems in our community.

Our country badly needs development. The hard-won political freedom will be meaningless unless poverty, disease and ignorance are tackled root, stock and leaf. The struggle to bring about peace is not an easy one. The struggle to bring about development is also not going to be an easy one. It is going to need people with courage and dedication to get it off the ground.

It is imperative that we bring an end to the violence as a matter of urgency as there can be no meaningful development in a climate of violence. So peace and development go hand-in-hand and therefore the challenge that remains is for a comprehensive awareness campaign so that people could understand this as well.

We need to strengthen our social institutions, the family, the church and the school so that they too could begin to make a difference in our society for peace and development.

The fostering of attitudes for development in a transition to democracy

Rev. Griffiths Malaba

A leader in education, administration, business and church, Zimbabwe

Abstract

This paper contends that the population as a whole must play a central role in the transition to democratic rule. This involves examining the role of culture, the media and youth on the birth of democracy. There must be free debate on the concept of democracy in order to see how democracy can speak to the African personality.

The culture of fear, silence and subservience which threatens the development of attitudes which foster the development of the new democracies, must be addressed squarely.

The politician's catchment area for votes is the women's league. Therefore it is incumbent upon all of us to ensure that women in rural areas are equipped to vote intelligently.

As representative democracy is preferable to other forms of government, it is incumbent upon us to design programmes to educate the populace in democratic rule and the importance of democratic structures at every level.

The subject of this paper is "The fostering of attitudes for development in a transition to democracy". This paper will attempt to share with you the salient attitudinal, cultural and conceptional challenges in the transition from oligarchies, one party democracies and non-democratic rule to representative democracy.

Political context

In his independence message on the 17th of April 1980, the then Prime Minister of Zimbabwe said:

"Independence will bestow on us a new personality, a new future and perspective, and indeed a new history. Our nation requires of everyone of us a new spirit. If ever we look back to the past, let us do so for the lessons the past has taught us, namely that oppression and racism are iniquities that must never again find scope in our political and social system ..."

This statement encapsulates our political and democratic aspirations as a people who have lived with oppression under oligarchies and minority rule and who now wish to make the transition to participatory rule. Our experience is that non-democratic rule imposes partisan decisions on people who have not been allowed to express their view on issues that affect their lives. This is a violation of a basic human right.

The collapse of the Soviet Union, the ocean of refugees fleeing the tyrannical one-party regimes and inhuman rule, indicate overwhelming preference for a new social order which is people-oriented, responsive to their aspirations and which holds itself accountable to the electors.

Attitudinal challenges

R. Dworkin says: "The old order changes, yielding place to new – and freedom finds itself in disarray, under attack from new enemies among its old champions[1]." What Dworkin means, I think, is that we should not be under the illusion that the transition to democratic rule will be smooth – it has its turbulences and tempests partly because of greed and partly because power tends to corrupt and even octogenarians are often loath to let go of power. Non-democratic attitudes deeply imbedded in the social fibres of society are resilient and even when they have become irrelevant in the light of changing times, they do not die easily and are often impervious to arguments for change.

Democracy: the concept

Democracy in the western sense of that word is somewhat alien to the African personality and African culture. African rulers consulted their people but they had enormous powers to veto the views of their advisors and to act unilaterally, and had ways of expressing their displeasures with protracted debate. So, the road to democracy means making the concept of democracy western-style, culturally endogenous.

This means starting at the apex of our social structure, for the apex is the custodian of the status quo. The myth that when a ruler imposes his will on his subjects, dissenters may not dissent, must be demythologised.

As the church in Africa is grappling with the problem of contextualising the Christian message to speak to the African personality and culture, so democracy must speak to African social structures in the endogenisation process to avoid giving the impression of imposing Western values on African cultures. For democracy to be vibrant and meaningful, it must be imbedded in African social systems and social values.

The cultures of fear, silence, lies and subservience: the case for free public debate

The road to the new social order requires that we urgently address the threats to the development of a democratic culture. The culture of fear negates the unfettered development of participatory democracy. The buttressing of the culture of fear is a violation of a basic human right "Where violence reigns, man is reduced to silence." Silence is the death of freedom of speech and the result is subservience, especially if violence is perpetrated by state informers planted in public and private sector establishments or in non-governmental organisations. Africa needs to rid itself of the culture of silence which does violence to women's rights, effectively muzzles the opposition and encourages undemocratic and tyrannical government.

What we need desperately is free public debate on socio-political, ethical and social reconstruction issues, beginning at grass-roots level, to nurture the democratic spirit. "It is manifestly unacceptable that development and transformation in Africa can proceed without the full participation of its people"[2] in the decision-making process through popularly-elected representatives.

Role of youth

The youth have to be involved in working out the modalities of African transition to democratic rule because it is they who will live in the new South Africa. They were mobilised for a war situation. In the new South Africa their role will be to build and not to destroy. We have to establish a pattern of democratic structures at all levels of our society and involve gang-groups because the life of our youth is influenced by peer groups.

Youth do not have vested interests in the status quo: they can be mobilised and trained to foster attitudes for development in South Africa in transition. Whereas their previous training was for destruction, the new training should use the latent potentialities of the youth in the service of the new social order. This involves putting in place an educational programme devised to foster attitudes for development in a transition to democracy.

If we are agreed that democracy is preferable to other forms of government, then it is incumbent upon us to accept that youth can be mobilised to pioneer change in our society.

K. Mannheim says: "... static societies which develop only gradually, and in which the rate of change is relatively low, will rely mainly on the experience of the old. They will be reluctant to encourage the new potentialities latent in the young. Their education will be focussed on the transfer of tradition, their methods of teaching will be reproductive and repetitive. The vital and spiritual reserves of youth will be deliberately neglected, as there is no will to break with the existing tendencies in society."[3]

The police

The police have a vital role in the maintenance of law and order. The new police force which will hopefully be people-oriented will need re-education in the new social order – to be trained to regard itself as a service to the people and not primarily a law enforcement arm of government. Such training should focus on attitudinal changes so that the police force can show professionalism in its approach to crime, and not disregard human rights issues in its day-to-day activities. When a police officer uses unprofessional investigative methods, he brings the service into disrepute. In other words the police must appreciate the fact that they have to be non-partisan in carrying out their duties. Above all, the police force must be human rights oriented.

The role of culture in development

Some cultures regard themselves as sacrosanct and create a mental climate which discourages experimentation. Consequently the role of women in development is underplayed, and the tragedy is that the social values which shape relations, which are a reflection of cultural assumptions about interpersonal relations, "then assume a level which is inaccessible to exploration, reflection and discussion".

In some parts of Africa a simple activity like when to plough has to be viewed in a traditional context. So the incentive to do better than your neighbour is not there. Such practices retard progress and development.

Development is endogenous, it can only come from within the society and a people, and depends on the internal strengths and cooperation of the people of that society. As such we Africans have to realise that we can only have development by accepting that we are the ones to achieve it: it will never come from abroad.

There is always a cultural dimension in development. Culture is an integral part of development. Culture is inseparable from development. Development that ignores the moral and spiritual values of a people cannot guarantee their survival over time. Development that has no respect for human values is empty. What would be the use of development if it ignored the cultural values on which all progress depends. What would man achieve if development did not enhance the value and quality of life. There can be no genuine development without taking the cultural dimension into account.

Christian values such as mutual assistance and cooperation, unity, generosity, community sharing are central to national development. Cultural values that prevent the transfer of knowledge and technology for development should be examined and transformed.

Development can be affected negatively by culturally conditioned attitudes towards new ideas. We are all products of our cultural environments. Our attitudes, our responses and our values are profoundly influenced by the customs, beliefs and practices of our society.

In broad terms African culture is not time-conscious. Punctuality and adhering to schedules seem somewhat alien. To trade with the rest of the world, we have to assure our markets that our products will arrive on time, that the quality will be as specified in trade agreements and that we are totally dependable as entrepreneurs. So, to get into the mainstream of development, our people must be time-conscious – must be taught to budget their time. Failure to do this, will result in diminishing productivity. We must reject those aspects of our culture which are a hindrance to development.

We should nurture a new work ethic at the workplace – absolute honesty. There are workers who want to earn more and more money for less and less work. Negative worker attitudes frustrate the establishment of democracy in industry and commerce. Profit-sharing schemes are intended to motivate workers and to enable them to realise that the establishment is theirs.

The role of the media

The media has a central role in forming public opinion. Those who control the media can inform, misinform and disinform the public resulting in greater concentration of power in the hands of the few. In the run-up to elections government controlled media have to be seen to be impartial in their coverage of election campaigns and ensure that the fundamental rights of voters and candidates to freedom of information and expression are not violated. "There is no viable democracy without an authentic culture of democracy based on civic spirit, tolerance, education and free circulation of ideas and people."

If it is true that countries cannot be built without the full participation of the people, then it is incumbent on us to educate the people for democracy. This would entail reaching all the women in particular, literate or illiterate, in the country to educate them on why they should vote.

Finally, I quote from a UNESCO paper: "Democracy for development must be based on the free and active participation of the people. A real culture of democracy must be anchored in the mentalities and behaviour patterns of those who govern and those who are governed. The need for democratisation in Africa must not be limited to civil and political aspects; it must also concern the economy, culture and society."

Recommendations

We recommend as follows:
* that countries which are on the road to democracy be assisted to create a culture of democracy based on tolerance;
* that education as one of the social agencies influencing human behaviour, be tasked with redesigning the school curriculum to prepare our people for intelligent participation in the democratic process;
* that there be a concerted effort to eradicate illiteracy to enable the peasants to read and write and participate in policy formulation;
* that youth be regarded as a resource in the transition to democracy;
* that youth wings of political parties be encouraged to have combined meetings to create a culture of dialogue;
* that the media disseminate accurate and impartial information;
* that where media are controlled by government, media staff must ensure that their reporting is non-partisan.

References

1. Dworkin R. 1994. *Index on Censorship*.
2. E/ECA/CM 16/11. International Conference on Popular Participation. Arusha, Tanzania, 12-16 February 1990.
3. Mannheim K. 1943. *Diagnosis of our Time*. Kegan Paul, Trench, Trubner and Co. Ltd.

The family at the heart of peace and stability

Dr Saths Cooper

Executive Director: The Family Institute

Abstract

In the International Year of the Family it is appropriate to locate the smallest unit of society, the family, as the building block on which peace, stability and democracy may be rooted in South Africa. This presentation, in adopting an interdisciplinary approach to the area, will critically examine key factors promoting and militating against peace, stability and democracy in South Africa, and will focus on family-centredness.

I am going to be sharing with you some thoughts which some of my colleagues here have heard but which I shall mention because it is very significant that we are having this gathering during this International Year of the Family.

The theme for this meeting is very appropriate to this burgeoning democracy that we have in South Africa. On 27 April 1994 the world stood still and watched the drama unfolding: of long never-ending queues of patient people waiting to vote for the first time. People who waited for the ability to participate in creating a new future, in establishing a new nation, black and white, rich and poor, urban and rural, all sizes; people from varying backgrounds participating in making this country happen in the fashion it has since that time. I believe that a new spirit of reconciliation was actually grounded on that day. Unfortunately, that spirit has not really been capitalised on by our leadership. It is a spirit born of tremendous wells of patience, of paths that have at times seemed overwhelming, but it is a spirit that may not last if certain things are not done very quickly to make people feel part of this change. It is very significant as well that this is the only country in the world to have adopted a new constitution this year. It is not a final constitution. Interim and flawed as it is, ours is the only country in the world to have adopted a new constitution.

It is also very significant that this year is the International Year of the Family, but nowhere in that constitution is there any mention made of family. And many of us debated this. Why is it that we don't have any mention of family? And we thought, well, maybe the architects of the constitution tried to avoid any definitional narrowness. Tried to avoid the pitfall of varying views and perceptions of what constitutes family. But we, after speaking to one or two of those people, realised that actually there was a political compact which paid very little attention to the issue of family. We would like to say that it is a grave mistake because a building block of any nation is its ultimate unit. Besides the individual, the next unit – and the unit of stability – is family, however you define it. Whether you define it in the nuclear context, whether you define it in the extended or any other type or form – family is the base of society.

Indeed, given the past from which we have come, it is remarkable that we have the institution of the family existing, tenuous as it is, in South Africa. It is remarkable that the family is still able to be the repository of its culture, of its expression, of its will and need. I am saying this because perhaps we have reinvented many things from the past which may actually militate against creating that future of peace, security, stability, growth, prosperity that all of us cherish.

If we look, for instance, at the welter of government ministries we have: all of them, with the possible exception of the RDP ministry, are concerned with deficit, with problems. Nowhere, save for a part of Welfare, do we have a ministry dealing with people, with human services, human development and enablement of people. And if we are talking about most people in our society and where they would be covered, besides births and deaths, it is within the sphere of welfare. But are we a nation doomed to be welfare recipients only? Are we a nation that will continue the cycle of dependency, created in the past where very little enablement happened for citizens? The past power structure can rear itself in the present and the future. The old rigid hierarchies of top-down are very easy for new rulers, for anybody, to just fall into and continue doing. Some of us have said it is very easy to move from the "meneer" mentality to change it around to say "comrade", but still the hierarchies remain. Still the top-down approach, and very little else starts shifting.

If we look at the eruptions across our country, economic and other, analysts have said that there have been fewer strikes this year than in a comparable period last year and so on. Such analysis is actually missing some of the "expectation of delivery" aspects. If we look at the heightened crime reported in statistics some people will say, especially representatives of the police, that indeed there is a new attitude within communities where more people are beginning to report these crimes and therefore we are having higher statistics. Actually the truth is that there is an increase in socio-economic insecurity and instability in our society.

Transition is not an easy time. It hasn't been easy for this country in the last five years or so that transition has been afoot in a meaningful way.

Change is difficult for the best of us to accustom ourselves to. To get accustomed to this auditorium and find the toilets which may be inconveniently placed, means an adjustment. But the adjustment that our society has seen and that particularly the majority of citizens who are young people have seen, entire nations and epochs in history haven't seen in such a concentrated fashion. And that is the background in which our children are growing. Growing to see the images portrayed of destruction, of self-immolation, of response to the other that can be an aggrieved response.

Many, many of our young children in townships and in rural areas across our country are exposed to a veritable culture of violence – which violence I believe has been endemic in our society over a long period of time. That violence is not simply a phenomenom following the 2nd of February 1990, but it is an essential and intrinsic part of this society. Most of us, whether we are black or white, have grown up to accept the correctness of responding in some violent manner to somebody else because we have seen significant authority figures exercise violence. Consider our child-rearing practices. Perhaps we are one of the few societies in the world that relies on the type of child-rearing practices that we take for granted. Especially in North America and Western Europe, if we were to do to our children what many of us in South Africa do – not just a particular group or a particular class but nearly all of us do – most of us would have our kids taken away from us and put in the department of Social Services' custody. We do not hesitate to lift our hands the moment that child does something which we don't have the time, energy, perhaps the patience, to understand and deal with.

I will give you an example that some of my colleagues may have already heard. Suppose we are in a gathering like this and our children are around and one child beats another child up or they are playing and the child gets hurt. The child is going to scream. Children scream when they are hurt. And children bleed very easily as well. So before you know it there is blood dribbling from the corner of the child's mouth and if it is my child that's somehow been responsible for creating this unfortunate incident I will rush up there. Everybody will be uptight. And I am immediately – split second – thinking, what are these people thinking about me? It is my child who has beaten this other child up and I scream "Why have you done this?" The tone of voice is already violent. The little child is half a metre high and the adult is three to four times taller, and the child is seeing the world from that perspective, with this huge figure looming large and threatening. And I yank that child – already another act of violence – and I start shaking the child – and I say "Why did you do this?" – further violence – and, heaven forbid, I say "I told you not to do that" and go ahead and use my hand on the child. A mixed message! I am doing exactly what my child did to the other child and I am saying I told you not to do that. This child is unable to integrate that. Developmentally the child doesn't have (most of us in the society don't have) the ingredients to integrate that behaviour and step back to think "I must distinguish what my parent is doing to me from what I did to this other child". The child doesn't have the ability to categorise in that fashion. Developmentally, psychologically, emotionally, physically that child is not made up to understand it in that way. But that is how most of us have been brought up. Very few of us have been brought up in this country without experiencing physical chastisement. Black, white, urban, rural, rich, poor, that is how we have done it.

And the violence has been quite dramatic: the public violence that has been covered in our media from 1990 especially. But you well know that the public violence preceded February 1990 – it was just that the censorship laws were lifted after that, creating the awareness of what we are doing to each other; of what we are doing to ourselves – individuals, groups, factions, and whoever else.

But I believe that, during that period and especially now, the violence that has been higher than the political violence in terms of real statistics, is interpersonal violence. It has been within the home, within the social environment. That fact has to be acknowledged. More people have done grievous bodily injury to other people in social and familial contexts in our society. Right now, and members of the Department of Welfare will bear me out on it, the statistics are going above the roof. Spouse battering, children abuse, rape, the murder rate in this country; the police report serious injury to people high amongst their reporting statistics every quarter or so. It tells us something about the ingredients that exist in our society. I merely have to drive down the street and when that traffic light turns from red to green and I don't move my car quickly enough into the intersection, I've got quite a few irate drivers honking away behind me, and if I happen to turn around and expostulate I can get shot. It tells you something. Our accident rate is higher proportionally than anywhere else in the world – all the indices classically of a very violent society.

And in this milieu we have a few men and women involved in creating conditions for peace. They are faced with a task that is almost hopeless, save that they are filled with a certain missiology, if you like, that is good, something that we need to cherish and hanker after. And that is why I believe that we need to go to the base of society and create those conditions. Go to that building block within the nursery schools, within the home environment and create conditions for peace, for stability, for people to understand each other; this nation that is a nation abused, that has been abusing itself, a nation divided tragically against itself. We need to make people relate to each other in ordinary human ways. And people everywhere have the ability to do so. But the world is too much with us and especially now – the narrow politics is also too much with us. When the politics interfere, then I belong to this "ism" and you are beyond repair and I cannot interact with you in ways in which I just dealt with you an hour ago.

Take any platteland area where there has been the notion that Afrikaners treat black people terribly – you find that people get on quite well. They know their boundaries – they have a certain respectful interaction – but the moment the politics, the ideological issue, interferes, the iron curtain is placed between them. Those are the things that happen. We need, in this transition, to be in a better place to remove the narrow constriction of partisan politics. It has in some aspects been enabling of where we've come to politically, but it has actually been our bugbear in this society. We need to be able to interact with each other as human beings and agree that we can disagree without attacking the person. But the messages our leadership have given in the run-up to the election – it was still a jihad out there. No political party can claim it didn't participate in that. Every one of our political parties stands accused of doing that. Very few of the political parties were able to exercise discipline over their individual campaigners. Racist campaigns, campaigns oriented at particular individuals, at creating bogies out of the other side. And then we have this marvellous advent: the Government of National Unity. It is delicious for the PAC deputy leader to claim, a month or so after the new government's installation, that anybody who attacks the police force is really beyond repair. But a month before, the message was different. I am not anti-PAC – I am just giving you an example. And then post-election you still have some of the politicians engaging in the same whipping up of emotions when they are faced with an almost hopeless situation, considering what they have inherited.

I pity those of you who sit as senators and members of different legislatures. I pity what you have inherited. Because it is not an easy task. But at the same time I will not hesitate to criticise you because it is my civic, democratic right to do so. Now when I criticise it does not mean that I am going to be attacking Carel Boshoff the man, because actually that is irrelevant to attacking a particular position. But we have not come to that pass in our society, so where do we start?

My belief is that we need to start at the begining. We need to start where society starts. We need to start where society ought to – within the family. We have not got a family-friendly society in our country. We need to agitate for family-centredness. The opportunity is available for us to do so. New ways of looking at our society are being created by our constitution, flawed as it is. We need to take advantage of the opportunity to participate directly in creating change. It is our right as part of civil society to make representations, to advocate better ways for enablement for us, not for any other people out there, but for us. Because it is our society and we are in this together, whether we like it or not. And very few of us have the ability or the desire to hop out of this society.

If a measure of the responsiveness, the caring, the humaneness existent in any society, is determined by what that society does for its most disadvantaged and underprivileged populations, then South Africa is a society that will come very short. And in terms of that disadvantage there are four major populations that stand out. *Children* – they are the bulk of our society. They play no role in decision making, resource allocation, policy, legislation. People who are *physically and mentally challenged* – those that we would wish to hide away – they're a significant population and also playing no role whatsoever in policy, resource determination, decision making. *Senior citizens* – thankfully we have some of the aged we do have in government and maybe there will be a new sensibility emerging for senior citizens. But very few societies are oriented towards the older generation. And then, *women*. Except for some concessions that have been made within certain political parties and gender commissions and so on that are being created, women in our society, especially, have played very little if any role in decision making, resource allocation, and policy. And if we use those four populations as a measure, South Africa is really to be pitied. We need to turn around this society, even when recognising that the problems are immense: over 50% of the population being under some 20 years of age; at least 50% of the population being actually illiterate; one in two persons being unemployed. Those are veritable time bombs ticking away, waiting to explode.

1976 June 16th was a significant advent in our society, and since then and into the eighties many of us asked, are we creating a lost generation? But what our children, little children, are being exposed to now in that endemic environment of violence, will constrain us to say in five years, the lost generation were maybe better off! These issues look very pessimistic but we need to deal with them up front.

We can create a better future. We have to turn it around in such a way that we allow our families to be enabling environments, without getting caught up in definitional problems. The United Nations wasn't able to declare an International Year of the Family for a long, long period and they were only able to do so when they definitely side-stepped the issue of definition. We have different forms of family, different types of family in our society. We need to cherish them. But right now our legislation penalises the majority of families because many of them don't fall within that Eurocentric definition of family contained in some of the Welfare legislation. We don't have a basket wherein most of our people can be caught and a rehabilitation programme initiated for those people. We don't have a ministry that really looks at healthy people, looks at enabling them, looks at developing them, resourcing them. We're still caught in the knee-jerk responsive mode. That is the problem. It needs a little quick-fix solution and we'll move on. We need to start going back to the aetiology of some of the problems. If we don't create that environment where we work together for our country as developers, we will certainly perish as destroyers.

Notes

The church's contribution to peace in South Africa

Prof. Carel WH Boshoff

Member: Povincial Legislature, Northern Cape

Abstract

The church of Christ in South Africa is called upon to be one of the main change agents in society. This statement, however, should not be understood in a humanistic sense but as profoundly Biblical – an agent in God's hands to change the hearts of people.

This change of heart does not only mean that such a person becomes a pious believer in God; it also means that he or she dwells in love. Where the love of God prevails, peace comes to stay.

Yet, peace and justice go together. The church must be prepared at all times to have a socio-political involvement in the community. However, the church and the clergymen should not pretend to be political, social and economical experts; fellow-Christians in different walks of life are also God's representatives and must be equipped to be more so.

The church should not fall prey to ideologies, for example, the holistic view to replace unity in Christ, or a civil religion.

Social justice is pursued today in two forms: democratisation and human rights. The church can support these movements on behalf of peace in South Africa on condition that the whole scope of reality is taken into account. Minority rights, the struggle for self-determination of peoples, should not be disregarded in favour of a unitary, multi-ethnic state. Love and peace in South Africa call for the recognition of the diversity of its peoples and their needs. South Africa is still in transition.

The church of Christ is called upon to act as a change agent in this world; not, however, in a political or even revolutionary sense, but in the sense of being delegates to change the world according to its mission: "Go ye therefore and teach all nations, baptising them in the name of the Father and of the Son and of the Holy Ghost: teaching them to observe all things whatever I have commanded you."

Indeed, as Paul commanded the Romans in his letter to them: "Be ye transformed by the renewing of your mind."

There is no stronger power to change man's life than that of the Holy Spirit, of whom Jesus said: "That which is born of the flesh is flesh; and that which is born of the Spirit is spirit. Marvel not that I said unto thee ye must be born again" (John 3:6, 7). The expression "to be born of God", being mentioned five times in the first letter of John, indicates how profoundly the change in man's life takes place when he believes in Christ: "Everyone who believes that Jesus is the Christ is born of God" (1 John 5:1).

And this change of heart does not only mean that such a person becomes a pious believer in God; it also means that he dwells in love (1 John 4:16). As the apostle claims: "Dear friends, since God so loved us, we also ought to love one another" (1 John 4:11).

The mission of the church is indeed to communicate love and to preach a change of heart, resulting in a new life in Jesus Christ. And where the love of God prevails, peace also prevails. As Paul assured the Philippians: "And the peace of God, which passeth all understanding, shall keep your hearts and minds through Christ Jesus" (Phil. 4:7).

However, love and peace do not represent an attitude of hear no evil, see no evil and speak no evil; for the love of God is also a love of righteousness, and peace prevails together with justice. The church, therefore, has a prophetic task and such concepts as salvation and liberation should also be conveyed in their broadest meaning: both as spiritual and tangible physical manifestations. The church, thus, has a daunting task of interpreting the major trends in the world and the country correctly, by anticipating the prophetic moment to be able to counteract by well-grounded responses. This also represents a true biblical image of the church. As the prophet Micah said: "With what shall I come before the Lord and bow down before the exalted God? Shall I come before him with burnt offerings, with calves a year old? Will the Lord be pleased with thousands of rams, with ten thousand rivers of oil? Shall I offer my firstborn for my transgression, the fruit of my body for the sin of my soul? He has showed you, o man, what is good. And what does the Lord require of you? To act justly and to love mercy and to walk humbly with your God" (Micah 6:6-8). The vertical relation between man and God cannot exist without a horizontal relation being present between man and his fellow-man. The artificially created tension between evangelicals and ecumenicals, or between supporters of verticalism and horizontalism, has no biblical ground. While the church must not be partisan, it must be prepared at all times to have prophetical socio-political involvement with the community, addressing such issues as systems and structural wrongs.

But by saying that, the church should not be tempted to think that her knowledge of the Bible and prophetic role enables her to be the super political expert or infallible critic on economic, labour or social problems. In all those fields she may be the guardian for social justice, but not the expert to replace the professional leaders in the different disciplines. She cannot take over the political role from the politician or the economic role from the entrepreneur nor the educational role from the teacher. Also with regard to social responsibility, there are barriers against the official church body or clergy adopting a prescribing role, which encourage them to rely on the Christian professional to represent the church: the lay Christian who is an expert in his field and has also become matured in the fulfilment of his Christian responsibility. The church is not only the official body, but also the body of believers and they are present in all different walks of life. Towards them, the church's responsibility is to equip God's people for work in His service (Ephesians 4:12). It may be a temptation for "church leaders" to become the spokesmen in politics, labour questions and other social problems, while Christian social and political leaders are much better equipped to play that role.

Now, whether it concerns the official church or the church as the body of believers, there are some practical guidelines to follow in the fulfilment of its call to contribute to peace in South Africa.

1. Firstly, the following warning should be issued which may alas be opposed by the disciples of the new dispensation of our time. Beware of the structural holism which advocates that the unity of the church lies in structures, and that a contribution towards peace can be made by only one church structure. Of course, the structures of the church are important and no one has the right to break them apart without very good reasons. But in a time of holism and holistic ideologies it is of even greater importance to realise that structures serve the church and not the other way round. There is a need for expression of unity in the world and every effort of Balkanising the church of Christ should be resisted, but that does not imply that the church as biggest organisation, and having the most diverse communities and languages, is the church which obeys the call for unity the most. There are great differences in church policy and ecclesiastical structures between the Roman Catholic and the Anglican Church on the one hand and the Reformed and Congregational churches in their *ecclesia completa* on local level on the other hand. There is also the urge to adopt one church structure which will deny cultural and linguistic differences in order to obey the call for unity in the church, to the detriment of those who establish indigenous churches according to language, culture and psychological differences, confessing unity in diversity.

Living in a land of utmost diversity among the peoples there is a need for the recognition of churches "rooted in Christ but related to the soil", catering for the spiritual needs of peoples of different languages who can all confess: "How is it then that we hear them, each of us in his own native language? ... we hear them talking in our own tongues the great things God has done" (Acts 2:8, 11).

Church unity should be discerned from holism. The local indigenous church is perhaps better equipped to call upon its members to live according to God's will, and to obey His command in community life. However, it should also be recognised that the local church may become a champion for its group rather than ministering the Word of God as the two-edged sword in community life.

2. The second guideline should draw the attention to the South African situation in which the need for peace is growing almost every hour. We have become accustomed to the numbers of killings every day – whether it is in group or political conflict, or by killing police officers, or during house breaking, bank robbing, car stealing or labour unrest. South Africa has become a country of conflict and instability.

Political, social, economic and educational disadvantages are being given as reasons for all kinds of unsocial behaviour.

Juvenile delinquency, child abuse, woman bashing, crime gangs, are the order of the day and hatred, fear and rage are building up. South Africa is no more a place of safety to live in; not for whites and not for blacks.

And indeed, what can one expect where almost 8 million people are unemployed, without shelter, families are without food, and where man is without hope? Speaking of expectations – unrealistic and impossible expectations may become one of the main factors to foster social misbehaviour.

Social pathology in South Africa is not the result of only one or two factors. The historical, political, educational, familial and cultural environment of its people should all together be recognised and considered. The South African situation, in this sense, provides an ideal breeding ground for unrest and conflict and it is doubtful whether a short-term solution can be implemented. With the population explosion we can rather expect an explosion of chaos and conflict. For a government to start, or to take responsibility for, a reconstruction and development programme, is almost an impossible task.

What we need is a new start, people with new attitudes, people with new hearts. And that is why the church of Christ has been established. The church is not a place for escaping the world, it is not an overcrowded ship for a number of castaways, trying to escape the storm, to be taken up in heaven. The church is not a hospital for the cripple, a haven for the blind and the deaf, or a shelter for the fugitive. The church is God's mission to the world. Hendrik Kraemer talks about the apostolate as the essence of the church. Without a mission, the church does not exist. The *raison d'être* of the church is its mission. And Dietrich Bonnhoefer talks of the Christian as a man for others. The reason to be is to be for others.

In that spirit, the church could be the answer to the world, the new beginning, the hope for a new dawn. But the church, time and again, makes the same mistake by either mystifying its own being or its message, or falling prey to metaphysics. When the church mystifies its message, it is trying to replace its responsibility in this world with a promise of eternal life in heaven or to comfort the needy by promising them a better life hereafter. When it associates itself with metaphysics it dwells in ideologies in large superstructures which remain unattainable.

The church believes that attitudes and relations should solve problems. The opposite is actually true: attitude and relations do not solve problems; they only create the atmosphere in which problems could be handled. Attitudes must have legs. Words must become deeds and ideas must be put into practice. The preacher must be followed by the politician and both must be filled by the Holy Spirit. And the Spirit-filled politician should be succeeded by the planner, the technician and the entrepreneur, and all of them should come to grips with reality. No philosophical or metaphysical solution for real human problems; no pietistic escapism for people in real life! No disregarding the realities which cause the crisis, no wishful thinking and denying of the facts! What the church is to teach its believer, is to face facts.

Let us try to do so, or at least to look some realities in the face.

Democracy

Peace cannot prevail when evil is rife, whether it is evil people or an evil system. To fight evil, two phenomena emerged during the last decades of this century. The one is called democracy or the democratisation of society and the other is in the name and actions of the Human Rights movement. The aim of both is a just society and both call upon the church to support the recognition and the realisation thereof. Because they are looked upon as universal as well as Christian truths, it is not difficult to understand why.

Worldwide as well as in South Africa, these two movements have made headway and won the support of academic, humanistic and governmental institutions. There is nothing wrong with that. But as with many man-made innovations, they have their defects either in themselves or in their actions.

In South Africa, democratisation has gone a long way and many believe that it has reached at least its first goal on 27 April, 1994. Human Rights is to follow suit and in the new constitution human rights will form the cornerstone of the country's community life.

The question to be answered is: How far has the process of democratisation advanced? After 500 years of colonialism we have come to the end of the era of colonial and minority rule. Even in South Africa the existence of minority white rule has ended. But is South Africa a true democracy? The question is how the minority groups in South Africa regard their own status.

In anthropological terms a minority is understood to be a population group which is largely self-perpetuating, shares fundamental cultural values and hereditary traits, identifies itself and is identified by others as a distinct community group or nation. The concept applies in particular to ethnic minorities in multi-ethnic societies, especially when they are exposed to discrimination and suppression. A minority grows towards nationhood through generations of intermarriage, assimilation and acculturation. A nation is therefore composed of people characterised by common descent and history, national self-consciousness and striving towards statehood.[1] Statehood as an expression of national self-consciousness and a need for self-determination started to emerge in the second half of the nineteenth century. Obstacles have been experienced right from the outset:

* Governments are not inclined to listen to demands for self-determination, especially not when secession is involved. About one third of the states of the world are in turmoil because governments suppress and persecute minorities, *inter alia* by denying them their rights of self-determination. The question is whether the new South African Government will be willing to recognise the demands of the Afrikaner nation and perhaps the Zulu nation and in due time other minorities for self-determination.

* Many dominant minorities govern as if their states were nation states and as if their interests were synonymous with state interests. Consequently, small minorities are accused of undermining the state when they proclaim their rights; and are persecuted and denied self-determination. In the name of peace in South Africa it is necessary to realise that the Afrikaner minority does not comply with the new unitary state. Are their claims for rights going to be denied or not?

* Insofar as human rights are concerned, governments tend to insist that human rights pertaining to individuals, such as equality, and freedom of association, also protect small minorities, thus obviating their need for

self-determination. Whether Afrikaners are willing to accept a Bill of Rights instead of self-determination, leave little room for speculation.

* Minorities can be frustrated in their efforts to achieve statehood by internal strife. Issues of principle or policy or leadership tend to divide practically every minority once it starts a so-called freedom struggle. Different parties and factions confront the multi-ethnic state with conflicting demands on the nature and the details of the state they want. Although their common goal may be jeopardised, they do seem to win in the end, as has been shown by experience in Ireland, Zimbabwe, Namibia, Afghanistan, Pakistan and elsewhere.

The new South Africa is in fact a multi-ethnic state. That sets the table for a new freedom struggle by different minorities. It serves no reason to call on Christian responsibility or a spirit of reconciliation among minorities in order to secure peace. The critical interests of people are to be addressed.

The vast majority of states just like South Africa have multi-ethnic populations, but this situation has changed considerably since the First World War. Several delegations from Africa, including an Afrikaner Freedom Deputation, attended the peace talks to complain about the oppressive policies of colonial powers, but the opinion of the great powers appears to have been that the right of self-determination applied to European minorities only.

In spite of this setback, the nation-state idea continued to grow outside Europe. Freedom movements multiplied; and self-determination was demanded as both a universal and Christian right. After the Second World War colonialism disintegrated rapidly, and many new states came into being. Few of them were nation states, but there was a distinct trend in that direction. The trend is continuing, as has been indicated by events during the nineties, most recently by the secession of Eritrea from Ethiopia in 1993.

In the theological field, the cry for liberation from oppression and injustice reached the ears of a new generation of theologians especially in what was the Third World church. That gave birth to a new theology, under different names such as Black Theology, Theology of Liberation, Political Theological and Theology of Revolution. Well-known people like Dorothee Solle, James Cone, Manas Buthelezi and Allen Boesak are followers of this new theology.

On the one hand the trend towards nation-states has also been manifested in Europe in the reunion of East and West Germany and in partitioning Cyprus, the Soviet Union, Yugoslavia, Czechoslovakia and Bosnia-Herzegovina. On the other hand, experiments with pan-nationalism have failed in these states as it did earlier on in Roman, Greek, Austrian-Hungarian and Turkish empires. Smaller efforts towards greater unity, as in Ruanda-Burundi, India, Ghana, Guinea, Senegal-Mali, and Rhodesia-Nyasaland have also failed.[2]

Human Rights

After the Second World War the UN worked relentlessly for the emancipation of minorities in colonial and mandated territories. However, the enthusiasm of the League of Nations for nation-states was almost completely lacking in the United Nations. The emphasis shifted from protection of minorities to protection of individuals. The Universal Declaration of Human Rights was drawn up to protect individuals against discrimination and persecution directly, and minority groups indirectly.

The UN recognised multi-ethnic states as an existing reality. This recognition rests on the assumption that if virtues such as tolerance and a sense of righteousness are cultivated, ethnic demands and violence will diminish. Minorities should learn to accept one another as equals and potential compatriots. Those who wish to maintain their identity can still be accommodated in one country under one government by means of a bill of human rights.

According to this approach, demands for self-determination and statehood are inherently evil and a fundamental cause of ethnic violence and warfare. Minorities, on the other hand, claim that persistent denial of self-determination leaves them no alternative but to break up the status quo.

As measures for the prevention of ethnic violence, declarations of human rights have not come up to expectations and have thus far had little effect on preventing or resolving violence and on improving the lot of aggrieved minorities. A bill of rights facilitates assimilation, the ultimate result of which is loss of identity. While this is not acceptable for minorities with a clear feeling of identity, the bill of human rights, with all its good intentions, has failed as a conflict-resolving agent.

The same applies to democratic institutions. As in the case of human rights, it was found that the introduction of representative government and other democratic institutions to accommodate minority demands and to eliminate violence, did not realise expectations. D Welsh refers to a survey in which it was concluded that there were only about twenty successful democracies in the world of which some were doubtful cases, such as Canada, Belgium, Malaysia, Fiji, Surinam, India, Sri Lanka and Singapore.

More and more minorities are looking beyond human rights charters and other constitutional devices, to secession as the answer to the problem of maintaining their identity. In recent years, attention has been focussed mainly on Eastern Europe, but ethnic upheaval is also present in Canada, the USA, the Middle East, Kenya, Burundi, Liberia, Nigeria, Zaire, Sri Lanka, India, Pakistan, Italy, Australia, Fiji and New Caledonia, to mention but a few in different parts of the world.

Democratic institutions have not prevented the emergence of self-consciousness and a drive for nationhood among minorities. Even though clashes of their critical interests may be absent at the start of a multi-ethnic state, these interests tend to surge unexpectedly and repeatedly. Clashes of a non-ethnic nature eventually coincide with ethnic boundaries, and demands for self-determination become unavoidable.

Prof. AWG Raath in a study on self-determination and secession quoted Vernon van Dyke who stated: "In the last few decades, assertions of another right have begun to appear: the right of peoples to preserve their culture. Perhaps it is better to say that a right implicit in the right to self-determination is being made explicit."[3]

There should be no reason why the striving of the Afrikaner people for self-determination should be condemned as less Christian, as international scholars convinced us that the maintenance of national entities is not un-Christian or undemocratic; on the contrary, the unity in Christ, as a matter of faith, transcends but does not abolish all temporal diversities, and democracy presupposes the self-determination of nations, so we should also call upon the church not to demand unity in and obedience to the unitary state as the only way to obey the Lord and the only way to contribute to peace in a country of profound diversity.

On the contrary, as the church contributes to peace by communicating love to God and our fellow-man in the new South Africa, it should also accommodate the critical interests of minorities who wish to maintain their cultural heritage in a land of their own. They should also be accompanied by the Word of God and by the Spirit of peace in order to achieve their aims in such a way that the world could be enriched by their contribution as a free nation-state.

As more and more ethnic minorities are moving towards self-determination and, in trying to attain this goal, experience resistance and suppression from the unitary state, they may be forced to use more violent means. In such a case the church should not be found lacking, condemning the urge for self-determination, supporting the status quo of the multi-ethnic state, not realising that Christians in the freedom movements also plead for understanding and support. Loving your neighbour in diversity also means to be open-hearted and open-minded towards minority groups and their pursuit of freedom. South Africa is still in a process of transition, and self-determination of minorities, such as the Afrikaner, is still to be considered. Attitudes alone can not solve this problem. Real Christian responsibility calls for the realisation of these facts and to recognise that need. If such an approach will characterise the church, it will indeed be a cradle for peace and development in South Africa.

References

1. Jooste, C J. 1991. *Grondwetlike beskerming vir Suid-Afrika se minderhede.* Pretoria Vryheidsreeks 5.
2. Raath, AWG. 1990. *Selfbeskikking en sesessie: Die saak vir die Afrikanervolk.* Vryheidsreeks 1, Die Afrikanervryheidstigting.

The church's task in reconciliation and harmony

Dr M Stanley Mogoba
Presiding Bishop: The Methodist Church of SA;
Deputy Chairman: National Peace Committee

Abstract

The debate about reconciliation has been raging for some time. The Kairos document put it very pithily: "There can be no true reconciliation and no genuine peace without justice. Any form of peace that allows the sin of injustice and oppression to continue is a false peace and counterfeit reconciliation."

The task of the church for many years to come is going to be that of enabling polarised people with deep feelings of fear, hatred and distrust to find each other and live together in the same country.

Reconciliation is a Christian word and concept. The world will never understand it if the church does not preach it and live it. Without reconciliation, the best promises, the best agreements, the best constitutions, will remain mere words without any meaning, without any practical help to anybody.

What is a church?

I have taken the subject 'The church's task in reconciliation and harmony', because I believe that the church has played an important role in helping to bring about the birth of a new South Africa particularly during the dark and trying times. The church is also destined to play a pivotal role in the future.

In very few countries in the world do we find a comparable situation where the church has risen to the challenge and has had such wide acceptance by the people.

But, *What is the church?* The root meanings and historical contexts show that the church can be understood in many possible ways. It could refer to buildings which are very prominent in our streets – we even have 'Church Street' in many of our towns and cities. 'Church' could refer to the faith community – people called by God to worship Him and to obey Him through the ministry of Jesus Christ and by the Holy Spirit. One root meaning from the Hebrew word 'Qahal' emphasises "the calling" – the clarion call – to people to gather for a crisis like war or for some civil action. This concept is closer to the calling of this Conference, the Peace Conference or the Rustenburg Church Conference in 1990. One of the concepts of the church in 'Interpreter Dictionary of the Bible' is that of the 'new humanity'. The church is viewed as the beginning of a new creation, a new humanity ... in

Jesus Christ all people are one through the fact of a shared creatureliness, a shared sin, and a shared death. In Christ people are transformed into a new people who participate in the fulness of God, the fulness of glory that is embodied in cosmic reconciliation (Col. 1: 17-20).

This is the ideal picture of the church. The reality is that the church is often its own greatest enemy.

It often appears as a collection of human beings with the worst human weaknesses in sharp focus in denominational racial cleavages. During the heydays of apartheid in South Africa, there was a saying which summed up the weakness of the church. The saying was: Apartheid is too strong for a divided church.

Bishop RL Speaks remarks pithily: "Powerless Christians are the church's greatest curse and Christ's greatest shame ... If the church is to become an effective witness it must be dynamic and relevant. It must be courageous and daring. It must dare to lead Christian believers into a genuine spiritual revival. It must dare to build upon the dunghills of hate; it must dare to build a new community of brotherhood, upon the shifting sands of racism; it must dare to build a new society of peace upon the wastelands of human strife. The church must dare to stem the tide of crime, drug addiction, immorality and secularistic materialism. It takes POWER: Holy Ghost power ... "

This observation by Bishop Speaks, made some years ago, remain true of the church today in the USA, here in South Africa, and in the whole world.

Biblical emphasis on reconciliation

Paul, addressing the Corinthians (2 Cor. 5:18), found the need to expound on the great theme of reconciliation.

This exposition by Paul has been aptly described as "THE CHARTER OF THE CHRISTIAN MINISTRY" – because it lies at the heart of the Christian Gospel: that God did not only remain loving to us but acted in love, emptying Himself in love – in order that we may open ourselves to His life-giving and saving Spirit.

Buchsel says: "The proclamation of reconciliation is the service the church owes to the world."

Paul in 2 Corinthians 5:18 wrote: "From the first to the last this has been the work of God. He has reconciled us human beings to Himself through Christ – and has enlisted us in this service of reconciliation."

GOD SPEAKS to us today in our situation – in our brokenness.

GOD SENDS us to our Governments so that as His Ambassadors we may enable "His will to be done, on earth as it is in Heaven".

GOD SENDS US to Africa which is being sacrificed on the altars of ideological expediency, maladministration, corruption and the crushing burden of the World Monetary System which are sapping life out of our

power-thirsty
food-hungry
dignity-lacking
fellow countrymen.

The church and bridge building

The ministry of reconciliation given to us by our Lord remains our important ministry for South Africa and Africa of our day. Politicians are too preoccupied with survival to have time for reconciliation. Most of the time they avoid each other like the plague. And yet it is only in coming together, facing each other, listening to each other, forgiving each other, that peace and life become a possibility. The church must build bridges (pontifex – bridge-builder, is the word used for a minister). These bridges must be solidly based on both sides of the river. We have too many bridges that rest fully on one side and are tied with a thin wire on the other side. Such bridges are dangerous. It is safer to swim through a river than pretend to cross over only to fall into the river.

The debate about reconciliation has been raging for some time. The Kairos document put it very pithily: "There can be no true reconciliation and no genuine peace without justice. Any form of peace or reconciliation that allows the sin of injustice and oppression to continue is a false peace and counterfeit reconciliation. This kind of reconciliation has nothing whatsoever to do with the Christian faith." Later on, another important condition is added: "No reconciliation, no forgiveness and no negotiations are possible without repentance."

Klaus Nurnberger and John Tooke in *The cost of reconciliation in South Africa*, while agreeing that there can be no reconciliation without justice, make this appeal: "The vision of reconciliation must be kept awake while the conflict escalates. Conflict has no value in itself. Nor has victory. At best they are means to ends. Legitimate ends are physical survival, justice and peace for all. Our children and grandchildren have to live in this land. South Africa must be rebuilt. We cannot afford traumatised relationships for generations to come."

Michael Cassidy in *The passing summer*, observes "It is a grim and glorious thing to be gripped by reconciliation in South Africa today. It is grim because too many white Christians see reconciliation as political and therefore to be shunned, and most blacks see reconciliation as cheap and therefore to be ignored. But it is glorious too, because it is central to the heart of Jesus, pivotal to the New Testament, and inescapable for South Africa."

My own position was made clear in a speech to Diakonia in Durban in 1981. The date is important to note because it is earlier than many of the current debates. The main points made were that reconciliation is costly, not easy; unavoidable (if we are to survive) and not theoretical:

"It means giving back human dignity,

It means regaining for ourselves human dignity,

It means sharing living space (i.e., land, not in 87:13 ratio),

It means employment,

It means parity of wages,

It means no more resettlements,

It means normal mortality rates for all groups,

It means universal suffrage,

It means release of political prisoners,

It means a national convention."

The task of the church for many years to come is going to be that of enabling polarised people with deep feelings of fear, hatred and distrust to find each other and live together in the same country.

Reconciliation is a Christian word and concept. The world will never understand it if the church does not preach it and live it. Without reconciliation, the best promises, the best agreements, the best constitutions, will remain mere words without any meaning, without any practical help to anybody.

Practical suggestions

Now, I must move from the theoretical plane of theological explication to the harsh realities of the situation that stare us in the face, and I make a few suggestions:

The prophetic voice

The church at all times tries to understand and express what it understands to be the will of God. In the prophetic tradition of the Bible the church must be able to say: "Thus says the Lord." This voice must be heard at all times, irrespective of WHO is in power at the time. Kings, princes and princesses, governments and people must always hear this word. A country with a silent church is a dying or dead nation. Naturally this word is not a comforting word most of the time. Father Trevor Huddlestone's phrase "naught for your comfort" describes this prophetic ministry. The good news is that, however uncomfortable, this is a word of correction, and it is a word of Life, not death.

Peace in our country

Our country has been in the grips of ethnic or racial warfare from the frontier wars. The name given to the river in Natal – Blood River – sums it up very aptly. We have unfortunately not had one "Blood River" but many Blood Rivers.

We have had alarming proportions of killings in our country. It is estimated that in the four and a quarter years from 1 July 1990 to 30 September 1994, 14 683 people were killed for politically related reasons. Statisticians agree that more people were killed after 1991 than during the war of liberation and independence, and that more people were killed in this country than in Ireland or in Bosnia. Something has gone wrong in the psyche of a people who, when truce is proclaimed, go on killing in a maniacal way. Nobody seems to know why violence is tearing our country apart.

This is where the Church must search for an answer. Our Bible tells us that only God can heal a nation that is sick.

Krister Stendahl in *Energy for life* uses three expressive words: Helplessness; Faithlessness; Powerlessness.

This situation is reached by a nation that has experienced the death of hope. Only God can save such a nation. Let us hear what 2 Chronicles 7:14 says: "If my people, who are called by my name, will humble themselves and pray and seek my face and turn from their wicked ways, then will I hear from heaven and will forgive their sins and will heal their land."

Or what the letter of Paul in Ephesians 6:10-17 says to us: "Finally, be strong in the Lord and in his mighty power. Put on the full armour of God so that you can take your stand against the devil's schemes. For our struggle is not against flesh and blood, but against the rulers, against the authorities, against the powers of this dark world and against the spiritual forces of evil in the heavenly realms. Therefore put on the full armour of God, so that when the day of evil comes, you may be able to stand your ground, and after you have done everything, to stand. Stand firm then, with the belt of truth buckled around your waist, with the breastplate of righteousness in place, and with your feet fitted with the readiness that comes from the gospel of peace. In addition to all this, take up the shield of faith, with which you can extinguish all the flaming arrows of the evil one. Take the helmet of salvation and the sword of the Spirit, which is the word of God."

The scourge of war in our land

It is totally inexplicable to me how the Christian civilised world and the Christian church have accepted war, or tolerated it or supported it or even blessed it! We have improved and refined our tactics, methods and weapons of killing. Instead of nuclear technology helping to improve the quality of life, every day sees us getting nearer to a nuclear apocalypse. Moltmann in *Creating a just future* remarks: "The horrible nightmare of the bloody final battle at Armageddon has replaced the political vision of the hope for life, freedom and justice."

Tim Cooper gives frightening statistics: "The whole world's nuclear arsenal is equivalent to one million bombs of the size of the first one dropped, which killed nearly 100 000 people in Hiroshima in August 1945 ... The world as a whole has 18 000 megatons of explosives today. In the second World War, 6 megatons were used! ... A nuclear winter can be triggered by the use of less than one percent of this huge global nuclear arsenal. In such an event the smoke, soot, dust, and other debris lifted into the atmosphere could virtually eliminate sunlight over the affected continents."

What a spectacle! No light, no growth, no heat! Two billion people dying directly from the bomb and another two billion freezing and starving to death!

That is why I called on the World Council of Churches Central Committee to introduce a Programme to Combat War or Violence in the place of the Programme to Combat Racism. Christianity, I said, had compromised with war for far too long:

War is barbaric,

War is evil,

War is contrary to the will of God,

War must be outlawed from civilised society,

War must be relegated to the dust-heap of history.

The world's resources, both human and material, should be used for Peace and Development. The prophets Isaiah (in 2:4) and Micah (in 4:3) have said it all: "They will beat their swords into ploughshares and their spears into pruning hooks. Nation will not take up sword against nation nor will they train for war any more."

We are followers of the Prince of Peace, and we are called to preach peace and to be "peacemakers".

Development

One of the most awkward problems facing a new South Africa is the problem of the underdeveloped – the problem of joblessness, homelessness and hopelessness.

All the excitement of a new dispensation, a new land, a new South Africa, amounts to nothing unless they can be translated into better and fuller life for all.

That is why we all seem to be agreed that development is the new name of PEACE. We all have to learn the ethic of *sharing.*

Jesus, faced with a crowd of 5 000 people without a meal and with no chance of buying food as it was already late, asked his disciples what food was available. Andrew answered: "There is a boy here who has five barley loaves and two fishes, but what are they among so many people?"

Jesus teaches his disciples about sharing. Sharing does not only take place when we have abundance or surplus. No – it happens and even is crucial and critical when the resources are limited. Sharing produces a new feeling of belonging and commitment to work for the common good. Jesus demonstrates that when people share, more resources are released (twelve basketfuls are filled with the leftovers). The essence of this story is that Christians need to change their entire outlook.

Roelf Haan, in *The economics of honour,* writes: "Jesus points out that *distribution* goes before production. It is the community exercise, the distribution, that produces well-being, and not the other way around. We do not begin with twelve baskets from which each person may take a piece. First the food is distributed, in tense and faithful expectation. Then the twelve baskets are left over, as the economics of sharing is practised."

One of the divines or ancestors of our faith, Basil the Great who lived in 330 to 379 wrote:

"The bread in your cupboard belongs to the hungry man;
The coat hanging unused in your closet belongs to the man who needs;
The shoes rotting in your closet belong to the man who has no shoes;
The money which you put in the banks belongs to the poor.
You do wrong to everyone you could help, but fail to help."

Another quote of some worth are the words of André Gide, found in a 1970 edition of the *Readers Digest*:

"Complete possession is proved only by giving.
All you are unable to give, possesses you."

Forrester and Skeene comment as follows: "The pilgrim community does not settle down. The people move towards a goal, and their whole life and activity can only be understood in the light of that goal. On the way, pilgrims discover what it is to be a community, a fellowship of aliens and exiles seeking their true homeland and kept alive by hope. People on a journey travel light and must sit easy to possession. It is absolutely necessary for people to share. And the desert is not only a place of threat and danger, but above all a place of scarce resources. God gives enough for all, provided it is shared fairly. The church of God can help South Africa by pointing to God as our guide, our sustainer and one who has promised and will lead us into a new land, a new Africa, a new world. But let it not be forgotten that the church in this country is made up of you and your fellow Christians whoever and wherever they might be. You must be ready, with your fellows, to be new missionaries, new pilgrims in our new age."

The making of a people: is the school responsible?

Mrs Swayzine L Nance

Home School Liaison, Missouri, USA

Abstract

Our world society can no longer afford to plan school curricula on theoretical ideals that do not fully meet the needs of today's children. Children need more than reading, writing and arithmetic – more than science. They need the assurance that the foundation of their learning includes the elemental subjects of living. These are the topics of Life Skills and Character. The technology of today's world has by no means eliminated the need for these basic teachings. To build a curriculum void of these subjects is to send our children into the next century ill equipped and mis-guided. The devaluation of these topics in our schools may have already contributed to the loss of a generation.

We need people

The strength of any society rests upon the quality of its citizens. A democratic society is a political system where a great deal of power is vested in the citizens. Therefore, it is imperative for a democratic society to have a citizenry who are more than mere beings. They must be civilised people, willing to be responsible for ensuring freedom and justice.[1] This requires that they are people of character. Furthermore, these people must possess a reasonable level of social skills, which will enable them to function within that society. Character and social skills are needed by every citizen. They allow us to function and interact together in a civilised manner. Working and playing together, successfully, requires both.

Lessons to learn

Character is the collection of qualities that provide the basis for making sound decisions. Included in this collection are commonly accepted traits such as honesty, respect and self-control. Character is generally thought of as what distinguishes a 'good' person from a 'bad' person. Whether a child is born with the propensity toward good or evil is a universal question. Perhaps humans have an equal bent toward either, being selfish and self-centred or decent and feeling.[2] What is sure, however, is that a child needs a great deal of training to face the world today. Amital Etzioni agrees that babies show no signs of inborn commitment to morals or social skills, but must be taught how to be civilised creatures.[3]

The character of a person is guided by deeper personal moral values. These moral values are principles and ideals that are shaped by our beliefs and attitudes.[4] These beliefs and attitudes often originate from religious precepts and teachings. The moral values of a person are intertwined with the character traits of that individual. These combine to develop strength of character. People with strong character hold firmly to their beliefs. Conversely, people with weak character may know what is right, but may allow self-interest to prevent them from doing the right thing.[5]

Equally as important as building strong character, is the development of social skills. Social skills are life skills that provide the ability to relate to both the physical and social environment. These skills include simple rules of sanitation, basic nutrition, personal relationships, and resource management. Every person, regardless of his or her station in life, needs to develop good habits for living. Life skills serve as an equaliser in a society that is economically and culturally diverse. They provide a common denominator which allows people of different backgrounds to have effective interactions.

This is where learning should begin. Character and Life Skills are two very important elementary subjects. Make a rocket scientist or a neurologist, a bricklayer or a candlestick maker, but please do not leave out the basic teachings of character and life skills.

Who teaches?

Every child is born to a particular set of parents. In a perfect world, children know their parents and understand easily the kind of adult that they are to become. They pattern their lives after the examples of their parents. They also obtain the skills for living by observing adult actions. When life is as it should be, children learn good ways to handle relationships from watching the relationship of the parents. Children also learn other skills for life and living. They learn habits of good health and nutrition. They learn how to take care of their physical surroundings and to manage their resources. By watching good parents, children learn how to parent. Children emulate their parents and determine by watching and listening what is right and what is wrong.

Yes, children are born to a particular set of parents, but this is where the ideal story collapses. In the real world, there are not always parents around who hold themselves responsible. Responsible parents have nearly become the exception rather than the rule. Families are floundering and failing. Currently, in the United States, half of all marriages end in divorce.[6] Our children are in trouble. In fact, as Peggy Meszaros stated in a 1993 commemorative lecture: "The profound demographic, social and economic changes in our society and world and the resulting sequelae of persistent and pervasive poverty for youth, will overwhelm us unless we are willing to transform our system of human investment to ensure that every youth is prepared to be a productive citizen in the next millennium."[6]

More and more of today's children are facing the challenges of life with very little support.

Consequently, the things children need to know for life and living are learned haphazardly, if learned at all. No one is around consistently serving as the example that is so vital to a successful upbringing. Many children are treated like adults by the time they reach twelve years of age. The concern is not that they are too young chronologically – this may be a cultural factor – the real concern is whether they are prepared for adulthood. The French philosopher of the 18th century, Jacques Rousseau, would assert the opposite. He believed that, "if you could do nothing and let nothing be done, if you bring your pupil healthy and robust to the age of twelve without knowing how to distinguish his right hand from his left, at your first lessons the eyes of his understanding would open up to reason". Rousseau was unrealistic. He too, wrote of a world of fantasy.[7]

No twelve-year-old of today will be unscathed by the effects of society. Children today are not taught overtly by their parents, yet they learn much. Children are acquiring knowledge from a variety of sources. Dare we ask what they are learning? The facts reveal that in America every 3 hours a child is murdered, every 40 minutes an American child is arrested for drunken driving, or every 9 minutes for a drug offense. Nearly every minute, an American teenager has a baby.[6]

Surely, parents are not teaching their children these things. The fact is, children are learning whether it be overtly or covertly, directly or indirectly. Unfortunately, what they are learning is not, by any means, well serving to themselves or to the larger society.

Historical perspective

Historically, schools in the United States had clear expectations of character and morals. It is well known that the morals taught were based primarily on Judaeo-Christian beliefs.[8]

Then, as diversity became the norm in the United States, people began to question whose morals were being taught. No one wanted to offend anyone by promoting the values of one religion or culture over the other.

In the 1960s and 1970s educators, who were perhaps influenced by Rousseau's writings, began to promote values clarification and dilemma discussions over character education. These methods presupposed that children were able to reason and decide for themselves what should be their own values. The theories suggested that a child need only to be exposed to a broad variety of options, then they could pick what suited them best.[9] These left a great deal of ambiguity, no one was either right or wrong. This had become the age of the individual and therefore this seemed to many to be the perfect approach to values teaching. What might be true for one might not be so for another. Each situation was analysed as it arose. Decisions were based upon what was real for the individual at that moment and subject to change at any time. Speaking of values clarification, Tom Lickona states, "it made the mistake of treating kids like grown-ups … it forgot that children need a good deal of help in developing sound values in the first place".[1]

In America, this was the time of hippies and rock music. Young people thought that the Civil Rights movement had given legitimacy to rebellion. Parents who wanted to control their children were thought of as abusive. Rebellion became pervasive both in and out of the home.

When these "free-thinkers" grew up and became parents, they, naturally, used the same unfettered philosophy in their parenting styles. Their parenting styles encouraged the use of freedom and exploration for children. It was important to allow children to make many of their own decisions and to be able to speak what was on their minds. It was important that children were able to "find themselves" and to discover their own beliefs.

Parents did not want schools to teach what they had abandoned at home. Many schools just got out of the business of teaching life skills and character. Whatever they taught offended someone. They were ever in the position of defending their curriculum.

What parents did not realise was, while they were experimenting with a new method of parenting, "teaching by not teaching", a great deal of learning was taking place. Lessons from other sources were prolific. The explosion of technology in media had come to fill the void. Parents did not have to teach. Television, records and other media sources were ready and willing to do all of the instructing. The next generation had no concept of absolutes, no use for right and wrong, good and evil. This transition happened rapidly, because by now more and more children were having children. In America from 1970 to 1989, births to unmarried teens increased by 80 percent.[6] These babies have grown and are now in the classrooms.

Sharing responsibility

Today, in the United States millions of crimes are committed on school property each year.[10] Schools have had to resort to drastic measures. Some schools are searching children as they enter school buildings, providing armed guards to walk the corridors, and/or installing metal detectors at entrances. Other schools are requiring students to display identification badges or carry transparent book bags.

Who are we to blame for the situation that exists today? The young people today have not created their ideas and ideals from a vacuum. They have learned all that they know from someone. The responsibility must be shared.

Parents are responsible. The foundation of a moral upbringing is no longer being laid by as many as half of today's families.[3] Parents must begin to parent with awareness and purpose. Most importantly, they must become better models for children to emulate. Teaching in the home must begin at birth, and continue until the child has reached adulthood. Today's parents have come to depend upon the schools to teach their children. They have, in far too many cases, completely abdicated the responsibility of teaching to the school. Instead of using the school as an instrument to enhance or supplement learning, schools have become the expected source of knowledge.

Schools are responsible. Schools have changed their priorities away from practical subjects. Character education has been relegated to a now-and-then mention in the classroom or a poster in the hallway. Students' learning is being hindered, because they lack character and social skills. It should be very apparent that qualities such as honesty, respect and self-control directly affect a child's educational progress.

The media are responsible. Mass media have captured the hearts and minds of the great majority of our young people. In one f rm or another, media invades our homes daily. Children are overly exposed to whatever is offered up for digesting. It seems that, too often, no thought is given to how children will be affected.

Other segments of society are responsible. The church, for example, can and should be doing so much more to involve themselves in the lives of our youth. They can offer basic moral teachings that promote the establishment of inner beliefs and attitudes in children. Unfortunately, traditional doctrines confine many religious institutions within the four walls of old buildings. The people that truly need help seldom venture into these places. The church cannot afford to look the other way when the needs are so great.

Making a change

The statistics of juvenile offenses on the streets and in schools force us to realise that something must change to stem this tide of violence, disrespect, and lethargy that exists in much of our youth today. Parents must change, and schools must change. Every institution in society that touches the lives of children and families must wake up. It is time to recognise how important it is to the future of mankind to be responsible to promote character and good life skills. There must be a cooperative effort to help children realise what it takes to make a healthy society work.

Parents must take on the main responsibility using schools and others to provide support. Obviously, the schools are far too critical in the whole equation to avoid becoming a full participant. Schools are teaching character and lifestyles even if it is only by example.[11] There can be no escaping the subjects. Therefore, for the good of everyone, schools should be bold to teach what is good and right. Controversy is no confirmation of error.

Schools can teach character. The acceptance of qualities such as honesty and respect spreads across virtually every religion and creed, and there are other widely accepted character qualities as well. Teach what is accepted, this is far better than avoiding the subject altogether.

Schools must help! They can be instrumental in stopping the cycle of failure. The opportunity that the education system has to influence is far too great to allow schools to shrink back from the challenge. Schools must be in the business of people building.

References

1. Lickona, Thomas. 1991. *Educating for Character: How Our Schools Can Teach Respect and Responsibility.* New York: Banton Books.
2. Kohn, Alfie. Caring Kids, The Role of the Schools. *Phi Delta Kappa.* March 1991. 496-506.
3. Etzioni, Amital. 'Humanizing and Civilizing' Common Ground, Not Divisive Issues, Should Strengthen Character Education. *Educational Week.* 8 June 1994: 44, 33.
4. Greer, Peter and Kevin Ryan. How to answer the hard questions about moral education. *The American School Board Journal.* September 1989: 26-29.
5. Curtis, S J and Boultwood, M E. 1961. *A Short History of Educational Ideas.* London: University Tutorial Press Ltd.
6. Meszaros, Peggy. 1993 Commemorative Lecture, The 21st Century

Imperative: A Collaborative Ecological Investment in Youth. *Journal of Home Economics.* Fall 1993: 11-20.

7. Rousseau, Jean-Jacques. Trans. Alan Bloom. 1979. *Emile or On Education.* New York: Basic Books, Inc.
8. Lickona, Thomas. The Return of Character Education. *Educational Leadership.* November 1993: 6-11.
9. Callahan, Joseph and Clark, Leonard. 1988. *Teaching in the Middle and Secondary Schools: Planning for Competence.* New York: Macmillan.
10. Kilpatrick, William. 1992. *Why Johnny Can't Tell Right from Wrong: Moral Illiteracy and the Case for Character Education.* New York: Simon and Schuster.
11. Ryan, Kevin. Mining the Values in the Curriculum. *Educational Leadership.* November 1993: 16-18.

Notes

Closing synthesis:

The road ahead for the family, church and school in contributing to peace and development

Dr Keri Jones

Director: Institute of World Concerns

Abstract

The pursuit of peace requires dialogue and a common commitment to peace. Beyond the family, church and school as cradles of peace and development, are the wider society and government, but all are made up of individuals, and so one can also refer to the cradle of the individual.

Government's aim must be equity and justice to all. Political freedom is meaningless without economic well-being, and impatience in waiting for change in living conditions will be a challenge to peace. Government must attend to matters like maintaining peaceful relations between employers and trade unions. Integrity and propriety in financial matters are of utmost importance. Continuance of the peace structures is very necessary.

In society, reconciliation is needed in the art of living together. Restitution calls for wisely applied affirmative action policies. Improvements must begin with identifying, acknowledging and rectifying wrongdoing.

The family is the basic unit of society, but its partial disintegration calls for clearer definition. True moral absolutes have to be rediscovered by parents, and conveyed and demonstrated by them. Regarding the fear of intrusion of the state in child-rearing, it should be realised that correction via a smack is fundamentally different from the use of violence. Migrational labour is not conducive to the family being a cradle of peace and development.

In the school, education should be for all and should begin as soon as possible. Curricula should be reappraised, with the cooperation of teachers, administrators and employers. Issues that need attention include corporal punishment and wholesome sexual education.

The church, to be prophetic and relevant, must address iniquities and injustices, within itself and in society. It must enunciate kingdom principles and convey in lifestyles the message of helping those in need.

Individuals do not change their attitudes easily, due to the immanence of evil, but peace can come about in the heart of man through reconciliation with his Maker. The individual will then affect the family, the family the school, and the school can influence society, which in turn elects the government.

During the last few days I have sat with you and listened to people who have been personally involved in the process of peace within this nation of South Africa. Some have suffered imprisonment for speaking out concerning basic human rights, whilst others have, as beacon lights, made a stand for justice and equality.

I have listened to people with no apparent hidden agendas who have expressed their longing to see this nation thrive and live in peace. Many speakers expressed that, as a nation, you are where you are because of divine intervention. This was because when others expected the transition of government to be bloody, it was accomplished in peace. Many delegates believed this to be a miracle. This I do not doubt.

When listening to the various delegates and reading the feedback from the various workshops, I have become acutely aware of the enormous challenges that this nation presently faces. I have, therefore, silently asked that the divine intervention that you have spoken of will be permanent towards you as you face the next challenging phase in the establishment of peace within this nation. At the commencement of the conference, Mr. John Hall expressed surprise, which is probably indicative of many in this country (and may I say the world), at the rapidity of the peace process, and the signing of the Peace Accord on 14 September 1991. On that day your president, Mr. Mandela, said, "We have today recommitted ourselves to recognise democratic principles, to peaceful coexistence, to economic and social reconstruction and to the liberty and dignity of all South Africans. However, we are under no illusions that the accord is a magic wand. Our signatures alone cannot light the path to peace. Each party here has its history, interests, hopes and fears. This peace accord requires all of us to share one thing, a common commitment to peace."

I believe the president's sentiments are endorsed by most of South Africa's citizens and these sentiments are some of the main reasons for the convening of this conference. I do not share the view of one of the delegates who believed that the day of meaningful conferences had come to an end. This nation faces new challenges and this requires that people of good intent talk to each other without fear or apprehension. A conference such as this affords each of us the opportunity that, if taken, will allow us to ask the pertinent and relevant questions that we all face and to apply careful thought and reason before giving our answers to the complexity of the issues within the nation. The government faces its own challenges which will only be overcome by practical thought and wisdom, if it is to be able to present clear leadership for the people of the nation. This conference was also convened to facilitate dialogue between people who otherwise may not have had any desire even to meet each other.

In his keynote address, Mr. Bryn Jones gave five categories of main institutions within society which help protect the peace while the nation develops. I would like to take this opportunity to adopt his categories to help with this summation and then add a sixth category of my own in conclusion.

Government

The first category is that of government which should be viewed as a cradle of peace and development. Dr. Cooper said in his address that South Africa was the only country in the world that has adopted a new constitution this year. This in itself should be applauded as it has removed many of the injustices so inherent in the former constitution. Nevertheless, it needs saying that government is only a cradle of peace and development if it acts with equity and justice to all its citizens. Government has to make sure that all its peoples share the same basic rights and opportunities. Above all, it should make sure that it upholds the rights of the weak and the poor. Senator Zondi said that "South Africa has, for the first time in many years, a democratic government". This leads us to assume that all South African citizens have gained political emancipation. Whilst this may be true, we must also recognise that not all its people (the majority in fact) have attained economic well-being.

This in itself poses a challenge to peace, as people who have for so long been denied basic human rights are asked, once again, to wait a little longer before seeing their living conditions change. This is a great deal to ask of people who have already experienced so much deprivation. They believed that they elected a government that promised to give them change. I do not believe that they will be prepared to wait too long before they expect to see a delivery of the promises made to them. It is as Senator Zondi said, "political freedom is meaningless without economic well-being".

During their quest for a meaningful peace, the government will have to tackle major issues such as:
* How do we find a way for an equitable redistribution of wealth in society?
* How can we help maintain peaceful relations between employers and trade unions?
* How can we raise wages, therefore, without causing a domino reaction amongst other groups which could disrupt the peace?
These and many other questions have to be asked and answered.

I realise the government has an enormous task ahead and that much of the problems they encounter have been inherited. A tightening of the belt has been called for from high places and some in senior positions have taken a reduction in their salaries. Whilst this is commendable, for the many people who are destitute it seems a futile gesture. Sacrifices, whilst noble, are seen in the light of what is still left in the pocket after the sacrifice has been made. The government and parliament must give every indication of their integrity and propriety in financial matters so that peace can be consolidated. A growing civil service and a burgeoning administration will absorb finance which could be used much more effectively elsewhere.

For these and many other reasons, we should pray for those in authority to be able to make wise decisions, so that its citizens can live in harmony and peace. For these and other reasons I see the necessity for the continuance of the National Peace Committee in its regional and local peace committees.

Society

The second category that I want to refer to is that of society. Reinhold Niebuhr defined society as "the art of living together". This can only be achieved through true reconciliation within society. As we have heard from previous speakers, reconciliation has its own challenges. Bishop Mogoba stated so eloquently yesterday, "reconciliation cannot take place in ignorance". My understanding of his statement is that the wrongs that have been committed, whether by commission or omission, must be identified. Sadly, we understand and know that wrongs have not only been committed by individuals, but by groups and institutions, which is even more insidious. True reconciliation, therefore, can only be achieved when wrong is identified and acknowledged, and forgiveness is sought, so that guilt can be expunged from the individual conscience.

This may, in some if not many cases, have to be followed by restitution which is more than just restoring basic human rights. Restitution is far more than giving basic human rights to people. For example, those who are homeless should be housed, those who are hungry should be fed, those who are unemployed given work or opportunities to work or opportunities created by creating new work. People should be remunerated in exactly the same way for doing the same job, irrespective of their ethnicity or social status. The same standard of medical care should be available to all. This restitution, I believe, can only be enacted through wisely-applied affirmative action policies, especially in housing, employment and education. We must recognise that the improvements that have to be made in order to help harmonise society in peace and development, must begin with identifying, acknowledging and rectifying wrongdoing.

Family

A third category mentioned was that of the family. Many speakers at this conference have said that they believe the family to be the basic unit of society and, as such, its stability directly influences the stability and infrastructure of the society. Whilst I accept that the family is the basic unit, I also recognise that we are already seeing its partial disintegration in this and other societies due to the emergence of single-parent families through the high incidence of divorce, unmarried mothers, or the death of one of the parents through crime or disease. The latter will become more evident in this country as in others as AIDS takes an increasing toll on the populace, resulting in a growing orphan community.

Questions have arisen in the plenary and workshop sessions concerning the structure of the nuclear family. As a Christian, I view the normative unit to be that of father and mother with children who are their offspring. We must, however, also ask "Is there a role for the grandfather and grandmother?" Or is just the single basic unit of a husband and wife to be accepted rather than what we are presently seeing – a single mother with children, or a male cohabiting with a male or a female with a female? As much as I desire everyone to accept my understanding of the normative, there are clear evidences that not all of society is still prepared to accept it. Neither, may I add, have we ourselves at this conference, given an answer to what we regard as normative. I believe, therefore, that it is necessary for government, society and families to say clearly what they regard as the normal, nuclear family, as the consequences of an ill-defined family will have repercussions in the welfare, legal and domestic areas within society.

Other delegates have expressed that true values should be transmitted in the context of the family. I have, however, to ask "What are these values?" Whose values and in what family? In the past, society seemed to accept basic moral values as the Ten Commandments. Today absolutes are lacking, leading to a true benchmark being absent to test society's ethic and moral values. For the sake of peace and development, I believe that true moral absolutes have to be 'rediscovered' by parents who can then convey them to their children by word and demonstrate them in a lifestyle.

Some delegates were concerned that the family may see the intrusion of the state in the rearing of their children, for example, disallowing the smacking of a child for gross disobedience. This, it was expressed, could lead to the removal of the perpetrator of the so-called violence (the parent) or its victims (the child) from the home. This is already happening in some Western countries, due to the enforcement of their own human rights charter. However, I believe that some human rights activists need to understand that training a child in the way he should go through discipline and correction via a sharp smack, is fundamentally different from the use of violence, which can never be condoned. The jury in this country is still out on this matter. I do believe that the family should be a cradle of peace and development, for therein the children should experience the love, care and involvement of both parents towards them.

With this in mind I feel that, for the sake of continued peace and development within families and society, the issue of migrational labour must be addressed, as the results of such a practice are destructive and not conducive to the family being the cradle of peace and development.

School

The fourth category I would mention is the school. As an ex-school teacher, I saw personally how the school could be the cradle of peace and development. Whilst I understand that there are different cultures within South Africa, I was appalled and saddened to hear that about half of the black children in the country are illiterate. The fact that children live in a rural area should not mean that they are disadvantaged later on in life because they had no opportunity to learn. Education should be for all and should begin as soon as possible.

I believe that within education there will have to be a reappraisal of the old curriculum so that children are being educated and trained with the necessary skills relevant to a changing world. For the schools to realise success there will have to be participation and cooperation with teachers, administrators, and employers, so that a holistic educational programme can be adopted throughout the nation's schools.

In regard to discipline in schools, the issue of corporal punishment will have to be addressed by the government, school and parents. Also, school teachers, parents and government will have to decide what should be taught in the area of sexual education. In this area they will have to decide whose prerogative it is to teach such matters. Is it the family, the school, the church, government or all four? Again I would mention that in the light of the growing AIDS epidemic in Africa, decisions on wholesome sexual education and the way it is taught must be made and should be made swiftly.

It has also been stated at this conference that schools should affirm the values of the family. Although idealistic, it is my personal view that this will be hard to implement, given the different moral and ethical values held within the teaching profession and that of different families.

However, despite the negatives, I do believe that there is an enormous input for good into children through schools, not only from the teachers, but in the healthy interaction which takes place between the students.

Church

The fifth category is that of the church. This has been called a cradle of peace and development at this conference. I have little doubt, on hearing the testimony given by many delegates, that the church has played a major role in helping to produce the peace accord. Yet I find myself endorsing the sentiment expressed by Bishop Mogoba that the church had largely ceased to be a prophetic voice.

I believe it fails to be a prophetic voice because it has failed to understand its mission in the world, which is primarily to proclaim the gospel of the kingdom of God rather than any denominational doctrine. Sadly for many, the church has become an object of ridicule, due to what is seen as its hypocrisy over many years. Happily, within the nation, some individuals within the church have taken a stand for human rights and justice. For this they paid a high price. Tragically, the majority within churches remained silent. The church, I believe, only remains prophetic and can only remain relevant when it addresses the iniquities and injustices, firstly within itself and then in society.

The church is called to enunciate kingdom principles, and its people should convey by their lifestyles the message they have espoused. In so doing, the church will become a relevant force within society when its people feed the hungry, clothe the naked, house the destitute, give water to the thirsty, as well as visit those who are in prison. The message of the kingdom of God is the true alternative for a sick and needy society. The church itself, by embracing its message, should be a light to those trying to find the way in a crooked and dark world, as well as being salt to preserve society from moral collapse. It is only in this way that I believe the church will become the cradle of peace and development for the many within its ranks and those without who need its assistance.

The individual

I would like to conclude with the sixth category which I have called 'the cradle of the individual'. All governments, societies, families, schools and churches are made up of individuals who have their own individual hopes and aspirations. It was Mr. Bob Tucker who said, "We may not be able to change another person's attitudes but we are able to change our own." Alas, I have found on many occasions that I could not do so. I found that the cry of my heart was like that of the apostle Paul, who said, "The good that I would want to do I cannot do." This indicated a crisis within himself. Professor Nell described this problem as the immanence of evil and asked how this could be eliminated. Again the words of the apostle Paul come to mind, "Oh wretched man that I am, who can deliver me?" There is an answer to the question of the immanence of evil posed by professor Nell and thus a hope for the individual. Pauline theology states emphatically, "This deliverance can come about through Jesus Christ. Where sin did abound, grace did much more abound."

It is Reinhold Niebuhr who describes Christianity as, "A religion which measures the total dimension of human existence, not only in terms of the final norm of human conduct, which is expressed in the law of love, but also in terms of the fact of sin. The good news of the gospel is that there is a resource of divine mercy which is able to overcome a contradiction within our own souls which we ourselves cannot overcome."

The opportunity for this contradiction to be removed has been afforded by the work of Christ in his death and resurrection. Thus I maintain, peace can come about within the heart of man through reconciliation with his Maker, Creator and Lord. He then becomes a positive contributor within society. I believe that the individual's cradle of peace and development is the starting point for us all. It is within this cradle that we find foundational hope for the nation. The individual will then affect the family for good and the family can bring its influence to the school. The school can influence society whilst society chooses the government.

It is from this starting point that I see a great hope for the nation and thus, the fundamental reason for this conference. We are challenged when we realise that we can ourselves live in peace and harmony. As citizens, we must always remember the words spoken by someone far more eminent than ourselves. He said, "I require you to do justly, to love kindness and mercy and to walk humbly with your God" (Micah 6:8).

If we will apply this word individually to ourselves today, I believe it will reaffirm and establish the cradle of peace in the development of this nation.

Notes

Ubuntu!
Love your neighbour in diversity

This Declaration is organised as follows:

- **The message of this Declaration**

1. **Preamble**
   Initiative and mandate

2. **Background**
   Needed transformation: reconciliation in diversity

3. **The aim: peace and development**
   Interlinked, the alternative to violence and misery
   Peace
   – A strong commitment demanded from all
   Development
   – Rooted in a sound community of communities

4. **Cradles of peace and development**
   Where attitudes are shaped
   The family
   – The value of caring relationships
   The church
   – The strongest moral force; the reconciliation task
   The school
   – Equipping people with character and life skills

5. **Postscript**
   Acknowledgements: sponsors
   Proceedings volume
   Copies of the Declaration
   Invitation to respond

The message of this Declaration is:

"Ubuntu! Love your neighbour in diversity"

South Africa desperately needs reconciliation and harmony in our great diversity. Reconciliation depends on shared moral values and respect for human dignity. Hence people's thinking must be transformed, leading to decisive actions that put communities in motion.

The interlinked aims of peace and development are the alternative to even worse violence and misery than we have seen. Peace demands a strong commitment from all, and development depends critically on sound community life.

Attitudes which bring about peace and development must be promoted in institutions such as the family, the church and the school. These institutions are important cradles of peace and development.

The value of loving and caring relationships is reflected in the family in its various configurations. In the pursuit of reconciliation, the church and other spiritual communities are viewed as the strongest moral force. The school has a most important role in equipping people with both character and life skills.

Relevant objectives are identified to further these aims. The public are invited to assist in defining actions and targets, and in identifying key functionaries towards achieving the objectives.

The process will undergird the RDP, whose success is interlinked with lasting peace and stability.

1. Preamble

What we do now in South Africa will make the difference between peace and violence, between human development and misery. If this choice is not made soon, the opportunity may be lost.

This document is the statement of a position that we regard as extremely important for the future of our country - and for that matter, for that of other countries in the region; South Africa's development can significantly benefit the whole region, and even the whole continent.

This Declaration emerged from a mandate obtained from a conference held in Pretoria with the theme, *The Cradles of Peace and Development*. This event was a response to South Africa's participation in the International Year of the Family. The Declaration highlights the role of the basic institutions of society in fostering reconciliation and harmony in South Africa.

The conference was organised by the Institute of World Concerns (IWC), a non-profit organisation, founded in the UK in 1990 to stimulate interdisciplinary exchange on issues that threaten humanity, and to promote genuine moral convictions. IWC also presented a conference entitled *AIDS and Your Response* in November 1992. The two co-patrons for the latest conference were the National Peace Committee, which contributed significantly towards creating a peaceful climate during the negotiation process and the April 1994 elections, and the University of South Africa, the largest university in southern Africa, traditionally serving all population groups.

A national and international panel of experts introduced the various topics. The delegates consisted of concerned practitioners and opinion and policy makers from all over South Africa and beyond. Speakers and delegates took part in work sessions to crystallise the message of the conference.

2. Background

South Africa has become a country of conflict and instability, and violence has long been endemic to our society. Disparities which have allowed negative attitudes to exist must be removed; everybody's cooperation is needed to bring about change and to combat violence.

The miraculously peaceful democratic elections of April 1994 should not create the illusion that the potential for disaster no longer exists.

South Africa could provide a model of reconciliation and harmony in diversity for the rest of the world. For this, we must all embark on nation-building, symbolised by peace, reconstruction, sound community life, and development. *A transformation is needed, beginning with people's thinking and leading to decisive actions that put communities in motion.*

The success of the Reconstruction and Development Programme (RDP) is interlinked with lasting peace and stability. Therefore, we must foster the attitudes which produce peace and development. Attitudes are formed in institutions such as the family, the church and the school. These institutions, acting within an integrated system of physical and social conditions, are important cradles of peace and development. We need an evolving strategy on how to enlist their contribution towards strengthening our fragile peace.

We need *reconciliation and harmony in the great diversity of South Africa, based on respect for human dignity and moral values.*

The result will be peace and development, which together should be a prime aim in our endeavours.

3. The aim: peace and development

Peace

Without peace, full development is impossible. In South Africa's unique, kaleidoscopic mixture of rich cultures, success depends on having a culture of peace. Fostering peace is a complex process that demands a strong commitment from all.

Our diversity, which is a fact of South African society, can be wonderfully enriching. Even conflict stemming from that diversity can be creative, but must never be destructive.

The high level of both political and criminal violence in the country is unacceptable. The incidence of interpersonal violence is higher than that of political violence. One of the most profound cultural diseases is an attitude that places the highest value on aggression, domination and winning at all costs - whether in the classroom, in sport, in the business world, in politics, or in war.

Values determine human behaviour most fundamentally, and sound values should form the foundation of our new South Africa. The right attitudes include and emphasise the pursuit of justice for people of every culture.

Objectives:

Positive attitudes: Attitudes and mindsets have to be changed. Without a radical change of heart there may be less hostility, and even temporary peace, but no lasting solutions. For peace and stability to be achieved, there must be neither a minority dominating a majority nor a majority intimidating a minority. Tolerance between the different cultures is essential.

Conflict resolution and negotiating skills should be developed throughout society. These skills include:
- cultivating the ability to listen,
- expressing one's emotions in a non-violent way rather than repressing them,
- expressing needs in clear terms, and
- considering different options in a conflict situation.

Peace-keeping: A democratic state has the fundamental task of protecting and safeguarding the peaceful existence of its people. Peace-keeping mechanisms need the community's acceptance. Therefore the building of mutual trust within the community is essential.

Justice must prevail on all fronts in the country in order to enhance peace. Righteous peaceful measures are the democratic state's most effective means of protecting peace and security.

Practical plans of action could include:
- an awareness campaign to make people understand that there can be no meaningful development in a climate of violence;
- revival and adaptation of the peace structures to become peace and development structures;
- the establishment of a 'youth peace movement' to offer hope, security, life skills and vocational training to street children and marginalised youths;
- urgent provision for counselling the thousands of victims of violence who have been severely traumatised;
- serious attention to existing problems such as migrant labour, which is destructive to families and counter-productive to peace and development; and
- encouragement for people to learn another indigenous language, and thus promote good relationships between language groups.

Closely linked with the aim of peace, is that of development:

Development

Political freedom is meaningless without economic well-being. Economic and social development is essential to combat poverty in all its dimensions – social, economic, and emotional. All socio-economic policies and systems should be judged on whether they build or take away personal dignity and a sense of self-worth.

Of special importance in South Africa is the normalisation and revitalisation of community life. It is only within sound communities that people can develop to their full potential.

The effective functioning of both government and industry is closely related to the condition of the institutional fabric – the abundance of clubs, social organisations, unions and suchlike in the community. A community is essentially a community of communities!

Objectives:

The institutional fabric at grass-roots level must be strengthened in order to have sustainable development. People can mingle in a whole range of different institutions, where the values of thrift, self-reliance, mutual support and trust, and a productive work ethic are encouraged. This leads to a working democracy and sound local government; it also favours the establishment of industry and commerce and the enrichment of the people.

A strong work ethic must emphasised. It will be vital to the success of reconstruction and development, and will determine competitiveness on the international economic scene.

The role of culture: There is always a cultural dimension in development. It is essentially at grass-roots level in unions, clubs and organisations that cultural bridges can be built. To promote this, the institutional fabric is vital. Within the community bodies, the skills of free public debate on socio-political, ethical and reconstruction issues can grow. It is here where mutual assistance, cooperation, generosity and community sharing, all of which are elements central to national development, can be encouraged.

Cultural behaviour patterns that hinder development should be examined and transformed. It seems that lessons learnt in Zimbabwe (and related by a prominent speaker from there) can be fruitfully applied here. For example, the culture of fear and silence, caused by social pressure and sometimes by intimidation, must change; it prevents participatory democracy. Also, to participate in the mainstream of economic development, our people must strive to be time conscious, and taught to budget their time constructively.

The skills basic to development should be promoted on a wide scale. These are literacy, numeracy and an understanding of business and the economy. Such skills and knowledge enable the individual to find a place in the economy. Thus both youth and adult basic education should be emphasised.

The youth are a potentially invaluable resource in the transition to a stable democracy. They have to be involved in structuring the transition process. The life of our youth is influenced by peer groups, and democratic structures should be established at all levels of our society. Programmes and organisations aiming to provide the youth with opportunities to better their quality of life should be encouraged. Formal and informal youth organisations, together with the church and the school, should play a role in fostering attitudes and activities that will lead to peace and development. A youth peace and development corps could serve as a vehicle to deploy our youth constructively.

A common vision of the future from which all will benefit must exist for a sustainable development process to get underway. This has to include the promotion of justice on all fronts. People must be enabled to influence and participate in development which has an impact on their lives.

The media have a central role in forming public opinion and educating people for democracy and development. For this purpose the media should be non-partisan and disseminate information as accurately as possible.

In all of our striving for peace and development, people's attitudes make the difference. Where are attitudes formed? The following sections deal with this question.

4.   The cradles of peace and development: where attitudes are shaped

The family

The family is the smallest unit of society. It is the building block with which peace, stability and democracy may be built in our nation - regardless of whether it is defined in the kernel form, or the extended or any other form. Every effort should be made to repair broken families. All major social institutions help shape our beliefs, values and norms, yet the family is the most natural and basic of these institutions. The family impacts society more directly than any other institution.

Positive attitudes of respect for authority, responsibility, the power of decision and the value of self are formed within the family.

There is widespread agreement that the role of the family is essential to reduce risk factors conducive to violence, as unmet needs are often the cause

of violence. The breakdown of families is, amongst others, evidenced by:
- abdication of parental responsibility,
- lack of faith in and respect for parents by children,
- high divorce rate,
- teenage pregnancies,
- domestic violence, and
- child abuse.

Children pattern their lives on the examples of their parents and guardians. However, responsible parents have almost become the exception rather than the rule. It is difficult for parents to rear children in a society where vital institutions have been seriously undermined, and for teachers to teach pupils who have lost all respect for authority.

Objectives:

Family structures in our society need to be cherished. We must affirm the value of stable and loving family life, expressed in caring relationships.

Norms and values: Families need to assume a far greater responsibility for transmitting norms and values to children, instead of relying on schools and churches.

A family-friendly society must be promoted in our country and we must develop family-centredness. It is, for instance, essential that the constitution must mention and acknowledge the family. The relation between the economy and migrant labour must be re-evaluated, as migrant labour causes families to forgo a parent's presence.

Relationship skills should be taught to couples to promote stable marriages based on mutual trust. Stable families require hard work and perseverance to be successful in overcoming the many obstacles they face.

Parent-child relationships, especially communication, should receive attention. Children must be educated on family related issues, and parents must accept responsibility for their children.

Family violence should be combated by training each person to handle anger constructively and to seek timely help. Such training should be aimed at all family members, and must include victims as well as perpetrators of domestic violence. Loving, professional care of the abused should receive special attention.

Earning enough money to pay for suitable housing should be a focus in promoting proper family life. The government cannot provide housing for all, but should make it possible to work productively in a growing economy.

Workshops: Interactive community workshops should be convened, through which communities can identify both the traits and the skills that need to be developed to improve the quality of family life.

The media can be used to encourage families to use community resources and develop the skills needed for stable and happy family life.

The church and religious communities can also play a vital role in preserving and reconstructing families by means of parenting programmes.

1994 was proclaimed the International Year of the Family, but to us every year must be a year for the family.

The church

The strongest moral force in the lives of most people in our country is the church. The church community and all other religious communities should be characterised by love, consideration and respect for others. They should bring to individuals the inner peace that leads to peace in society.

The prophetic task of speaking on matters and in situations which require it, is of great importance, and such communication should provide both correction and direction to life.

Love and compassion must be lived. Therefore the spiritual community should reach out to those in need. The message of fulfilment and growth has the potential to create a positive approach. This message will stimulate development and contribute to the building of a dynamic and healthy community based on sound moral principles.

Reconciliation in South Africa is imperative. We cannot afford traumatised relationships for generations to come. Without reconciliation, the best promises, the best agreements, the best constitutions, will remain mere words without any practical meaning.

Objectives:

Character building: Character building should be restored. Evidence of a lifestyle based on a sound value system should be seen in every sector of society. True moral absolutes have to be revisited, conveyed and demonstrated to the broad establishment. Vindictive attitudes, from whichever part of the political spectrum, must never find religious justification.

Prophetic role: Major trends in the country and the world have to be interpreted correctly. Then the prophetic moment must be identified for responding with well-grounded statements and actions.

Relief from suffering: Besides ministering to spiritual or religious needs, the church and religious communities should meet the challenge of attending to the practical needs of the whole community. The intention must be to change the plight of the poor, the disadvantaged and all who suffer, by developing their economic and moral skills.

Economic enablement: The church and religious communities should also assist in economic enablement. Their buildings can be used for other purposes, such as:
- literacy, numeracy and economic literacy training,
- home industry,
- care facilities for children, and even
- school classes.

Reconciliation: The message of love should build bridges, and enable polarised people to find each other and live together. Reconciliation between people will be a major task for many years to come.

Justice in society: Righteousness and justice and their application to the issues affecting society today, must be promoted.

Repentance: Repentance, confession and restitution must be emphasised in attitude and teaching. This emphasis is a good platform from which to expect a stabilisation of the transition process.

The school

Schools are in the business of people-building. Their task is to develop both character and life skills. People of character possess qualities such as honesty, respect and self-control, all of which provide the basis for making sound decisions. Social or life skills provide the ability to relate to both the physical and the social environment. These skills serve to bring equality in a society that is economically and culturally diverse.

The acceptance of qualities such as honesty and respect spreads across virtually every religion and creed. There are many widely accepted character qualities. Children are not equipped to reason and decide for themselves what their own values should be, and they need guidance in developing sound values.

The process of guidance should ideally start as early as possible. However, many of the pupils in schools are already adults. Educators need to discover the best way of coping with their educational needs, including the shaping of their characters at such a late stage.

Objectives:

Common vision: A process should be put in place to develop a vision agreed upon by all stakeholders.
- This vision should aim at developing children to their fullest potential, starting from effective preschool development and education. An approach involving the whole person is required.
- Education should be based on strong ethical and moral foundations, and a code of conduct should be established.
- A culture of learning - the desire to obtain and apply knowledge - must be fostered in the country.

Parental involvement is essential. Parents must take on the main responsibility to teach what is right and wrong, but schools should be bold enough to lend support in providing a concept of absolutes.

School and community partnership should be encouraged and developed.
- The community must participate in the process of providing education.
- Schools are under-utilised and should become community-centred to include parenting programmes, adult education, sport, arts and crafts, and cultural activities.
- Industry and commerce should participate, for instance, by arranging workplace visits for children to gain insight into the environment in which their parents have to operate.

Committed educators are essential components for schools to make a difference. Educators must be deeply committed to their pupils and to making a contribution to the healing of our society.
- Teaching skills, aimed at letting the learner engage with the teacher in meaningful discourse, are needed. Such engagement develops the interactive skills needed in human development.

- Teachers should also be trained as effective facilitators of peace and development.

The organisational climate in our schools and classrooms should promote an atmosphere of peace and neighbourliness.

The curriculum must be relevant to promoting the knowledge, skills and attitudes essential to a peace-practising and economically successful nation. Curricula should prepare pupils to deal with the major issues in our society which impact their daily lives.
- Peace and development programmes, including parents' involvement, should be introduced into schools.
- Effective cross-cultural education is essential. Understanding each other leads to mutual respect rather than mere tolerance.
- Students must be enabled to face reality in the community beyond school, and their chances of finding employment must be enhanced. The curriculum should thus give them an understanding of the working of economic forces; teach the skills that make them trainable; equip them to deal with necessary issues like managing their money and planning their time; and orientate them to entrepreneurial and management skills.

Upgrading: Underprivileged, handicapped and illiterate youth should receive special care. This care should include vocational preparation and development of skills that may be offered in the labour market. Their nutritional needs should also be taken care of, as malnutrition contributes to learning disabilities.

5. Postscript

Acknowledgements: Sponsors
Thanks are due to various bodies and individuals who shared in making this venture possible. These include the co-patrons and the many participants in the birth process of this document - speakers, delegates, organising committee members, and others who spontaneously showed their interest.

The major sponsors were the Department of Welfare and the Institute of World Concerns. The assistance included support of the conference on 2 to 5 November 1994, and of the dissemination of the Proceedings and the Declaration. Other sponsors included Highveld Steel and Vanadium, Remata Bureau and Printers, and Southern Harvest Ministries.

Proceedings volume

A proceedings volume, containing the Declaration as well as the papers delivered at the conference, is being published by Kagiso Publishers.

Copies of the Declaration

To ensure that this Declaration has its fullest impact, it should be given maximum exposure and broad distribution. Further copies can be obtained from the organisers.

Invitation to respond

We invite responses to the contents of this Declaration. Participants in its preparation showed considerable consensus on the analyses and objectives outlined in this document. *However, greater focus is needed to arrive at well-defined actions and targets, and especially to identify key functionaries who will act to achieve the stated objectives.* For these steps, we need your help.

We would appreciate receiving your thoughts and details. Please direct correspondence to the organisers:

The Institute of World Concerns
PO Box 17177,
Groenkloof,
0027, South Africa.